BLUE

WATER

CAFE

BLUE

frank pabst

TEXT BY *jim tobler*

PHOTOGRAPHY BY *john sherlock*

enjoy the ocean
one fish at a time
culinary wishes
Frank Pabst

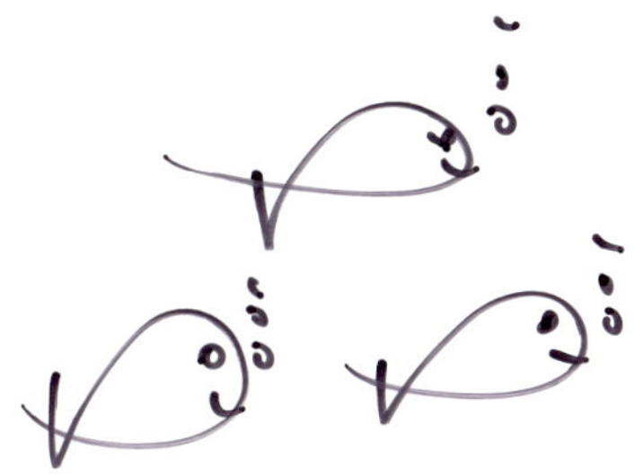

WATER CAFE

seafood

Douglas & McIntyre

Recipes by Frank Pabst and Yoshi Tabo
Wine pairings by Andrea Vescovi
Text by Jim Tobler

15 16 17 18 19 5 4 3 2 1

Douglas and McIntyre (2013) Ltd.
PO Box 219
Madeira Park BC Canada V0N 2H0
www.douglas-mcintyre.com

Blue Water Cafe + Raw Bar
1095 Hamilton Street
Vancouver BC Canada V6B 5T4
www.bluewatercafe.net

Cataloguing data available from Library and Archives Canada
ISBN 978-1-77162-108-3

Editing by Iva Cheung
Copyediting by Derek Fairbridge and Lucy Kenward
Jacket and text design by Peter Cocking
Photos on pages 4 (top right and bottom left), 8 (top), 10 (top), 84, 134, 163, 165 (right) by Brandon Hart
Photos on pages 4 (bottom right), 8 (bottom) by Peter Holst
Photos on pages 2, 4 (top left), 6, 7, 10 (bottom), 11, 27, 58, 77, 78, 81, 91, 111,129, 140, 152, by Steve Li
Photos on pages 3 (bottom), 194 by Jeff Vinnick
All other photos by John Sherlock
Printed and bound in China by C&C Offset Ltd.
Distributed in the U.S. by Publishers Group West

Douglas and McIntyre (2013) Ltd. acknowledges the support of the Canada Council for the Arts, which last year invested $157 million to bring the arts to Canadians throughout the country. We also gratefully acknowledge financial support from the Government of Canada through the Canada Book Fund and from the Province of British Columbia through the BC Arts Council and the Book Publishing Tax Credit.

Canada Council for the Arts | Conseil des arts du Canada

British Columbia Arts Council
An agency of the Province of British Columbia

Canada

CONTENTS

blue

BLUE WATER CAFE

THE NORTHWEST corner of Hamilton and Helmcken streets in Vancouver's historic Yaletown is home to Blue Water Cafe, one of Toptable Group's notable restaurants. It has a large room, now with private dining areas as well, and from the outset the idea was to create a fine dining seafood experience unlike any other. "Blue Water Cafe is multi-dimensional," Toptable Group's president, Michael Doyle, explains. "It's a celebration of seafood representing both East and West in a historic and vibrant environment, and equally, the restaurant is also about the true art of hospitality." The assembled team boasts a fine pedigree, intuitive service and a commitment to the freshest, most sustainable ingredients. The creative skills, energy and formidable organizational capacity of Executive Chef Frank Pabst make it possible for Blue Water Cafe to provide that fine dining experience seven nights a week.

Yaletown—so named in the 1880s for its large number of working residents from the railroad terminus town of Yale, most of whom moved into the then brand new city of Vancouver—was by the late 1960s a moribund place full of derelict warehouses and barren loading docks that had been teeming with railroad shipping traffic a few decades earlier.

Walk along the two main streets of Yaletown, Mainland and Hamilton, and you will notice a remarkable consistency in the buildings, almost all of which have retained their original brick and large-wooden-beam structures. The historic building that houses Blue Water Cafe is completely intact. This authenticity constitutes a large measure of the room's charm. The dining room has bones: the massive old-growth columns and beams that rise up from the ground beneath the building were installed approximately one hundred years ago and cannot be replicated today. The bricks themselves came to Vancouver as ballast on ships that were emptied of them, then loaded with goods such as lumber destined for the Old World.

Blue Water Cafe's executive chef, Frank Pabst, is one of Vancouver's culinary leaders. His career features tenures in Michelin-starred restaurants throughout Germany and France, including La Becasse in Aachen, Hotel Negresco in Nice and Restaurant de Bacon in Antibes. During this time, Frank developed his prodigious skills in classical techniques, which inform his cooking style today.

Restaurant Director Stephan Cachard notes that in a large dining room, staff levels and efficiency are paramount. He goes so far as to assert that "when we are full, everyone is focused, and it goes well. And Frank is always tracking to the excellent, pushing himself. It creates a team atmosphere where others do the same." Stephan is an alumnus of some of France and England's finest Michelin-starred restaurants: "Details are what it is all about in a Michelin restaurant. And my philosophy has not changed—the goal here is exactly the same: to provide a superb dining experience for our guests." That approach is never to be taken for granted: "It is all about scale, and you must have a team that performs well under pressure."

James Walt, currently executive chef at Whistler's Araxi, was at the helm when Blue Water Cafe opened. "It was an exciting time, totally new for the region. A fantastic experience."

Blue Water Cafe is a seafood restaurant, though others have called it "fusion." Frank does not use that overworked, ambiguous term. "Fusion is often combining things for the sake of combining," he says candidly. "We are not doing that." Instead,

Frank Pabst, executive chef

Michael Doyle, president of Toptable Group *Frank Pabst, executive chef* *Stephan Cachard, restaurant director*

Stephan Cachard, restaurant director

Masaaki Kudo, Raw Bar chef

Benjamin Wristen, restaurant manager

Adrien Boutet, restaurant manager

Blue Water Cafe presents a varied, interesting, sometimes even mildly educational experience. But the bottom line is, according to Frank, "the stomach and the heart must be satisfied. I don't want to go to an art exhibit or a gallery for my dinner. So, the classical takes from the contemporary, and vice versa." Fusion, then, means something specific at Blue Water Cafe.
It is a regional fusion—of Pacific Northwest foods and all of the ethnic food influences.

The Raw Bar, run by Masaaki Kudo, is the most obvious example of this kind of fusion. Kudo, a well-known figure in Vancouver amongst sushi aficionados, brought a wealth of experience in traditional and contemporary Japanese technique with him. He was attracted by Blue Water Cafe's commitment to the very best, freshest fish—all sustainable—and to Frank Pabst's dedication to utmost quality. "In our restaurant we spare no expense in buying the freshest, highest quality fish from our trusted suppliers. Frank and I have had relationships with them for years. It is always the best—there is no second place—and often we pay more to ensure consistently superior product: with sushi there is no hiding! At Blue Water Cafe, there are options—our raw fish often complements the kitchen's cooked dishes as starter courses, although many guests spend the entire evening with us at the bar. Frank and I collaborate every day, sourcing seasonally fresh product and discussing its preparation and presentation."

The entry to Blue Water Cafe leads to the main bar, and to its left, the guest's right, sits the Raw Bar, where Kudo and usually two or three other chefs are busily preparing dishes, many for people who specifically come to be treated by the master. A seat at either bar offers at least a sideways view of the entire main room and the grill section of the kitchen, flames rising and pots simmering. The preparation at the Raw Bar begins much earlier in the day, hours from service time. Chefs prepare various kinds of fish—maximizing the meat used, ensuring no bones or unwanted skin remains. They use special knives, each with its own unique purpose. The technique—cutting, cleaning and presentation—takes a long time to learn, about ten years or more. For Masa, presentation is at least as important an element in the culinary arts as taste. Perhaps that approach reveals a philosophical subtlety, but he lives by it. The quality of the fish, whether it is a local species or yellowtail from a special fishery in Japan, demands that he makes it look good, and then it will taste even better.

Seafood has its demands, its set of expectations on the part of diners who have, over the years, learned a thing or two about sustainable fisheries. Beyond the more obvious issues like the collapse of the cod fishery on the Atlantic Coast or the overfishing of the salmon runs, diners are more and more concerned about the long-term sustainability of ocean habitat. Frank has been a leader in the West Coast food community, along with some other dedicated, conscientious chefs, in promoting awareness and responsibility. "Sustainable seafood is not only about which fish you pull from the water, but about how you catch them and what impact fishing has on the ocean and on

blue water cafe
+ raw bar

William Mulholland, interim wine director

Colin MacDougall, bar manager

other species. We promote wild seafood, first and foremost, but we only take fish from people who we know practise responsible methods."

A fish tends to taste like what it eats, a fact that explains why the flavour profile of a wild salmon, for example, is more complex than that of a farmed one. Each species, then, has its unique flavour profile, but seafood in North America generally, for restaurants, has tended to fall into the main, obvious species. Frank decided to help diners understand that alternatives to the obvious choices exist. He calls these species "Unsung Heroes." "I use small plates and shared plates to introduce new flavours to people. We chefs have a responsibility to educate but also to be creative, make good matches for the stronger fish flavours."

This means, for example, that herring, mackerel, sardines—even anchovies—are featured in accomplished, inventive dishes that can excite both the seasoned diner and someone just dropping in for a bite before the theatre or the hockey game. "The recipes, the presentation, usually come from within," says Frank. "That is where the classics come in. Not necessarily to use literally, but as an approach."

In a fine dining environment, wine plays a vital role. Interim Wine Director William Mulholland explains that the traditional approach is not always what works best at Blue Water Cafe. "The original wine list at Blue Water was broad and very seafood friendly," he says. "Lots of whites and pinot noirs—French, American, Italian. But of course some of our guests wanted bigger, celebratory red wines too. And over the years, the burgeoning British Columbia wine scene has provided us with some of our most popular selections. Many visitors are curious about our local wines, and delighted with them—that section just gets stronger every vintage. We have also benefited from the legacy of outstanding wine directors at Blue Water, two of whom have been awarded 'Sommelier of the Year' at the Vancouver International Wine Festival. Our wine list now has great reach, and is far deeper than when we began." Bar Manager Colin MacDougall notes that "cocktail and wine drinkers are increasingly educated and more adventurous. Our guests suggest favourites from their travels and we're always happy to seek them out. The result is, I believe, a constant increase in quality, accessibility and value."

Cara Dunlop, reception manager, explains that the size of the room means that a smooth seating flow is a subtle but essential element in every guest's experience. "We need to work with the kitchen hand-in-glove," she says. "We need to balance the room gently so that the service flows gracefully throughout the evening—it's all about the choreography. And it's the little details that can really turn a good guest experience into something wonderful and memorable. So we're always curious if our guests are celebrating an important

Cara Dunlop, reception manager

event, or if the dinner is business-related and might require a little more privacy. Reservation information is a vital key and it's a good thing that I'm naturally a curious person!" Cara says.

From first contact to the final good night, the Blue Water Cafe team is dedicated to maximizing the dining experience for each individual. At the end of the evening, usually, are the creations of Pastry Chef Jean-Pierre Sanchez. J.-P.'s extensive training and experience—much of it in some of the grand hotels of Europe—mean he brings a great deal of technique and perfectionism to his profession. "We try to be local as much as possible," J.-P. says. "That means, though, that we can have fresh raspberries, for example, only three months of the year. And the focus is always fresh, not heavy—even in winter." He contemplates the size of the room and admits, "Even the daily bread preparation and baking is a big job." His overall idea, though, is that "this is an ideal room for fine pastry. Hotels, which traditionally are the best place for such work, now have stiff competition. As for size, in my mind, it is easier to do fine pastry service for one hundred people than it is for only two. Degree of difficulty is based on the team you have, and we never wait for challenges—we anticipate them."

For Frank and the entire team, the self-fulfilling prophecy is the expectation of excellence. When Frank was named *The Georgia Straight*'s Chef of the Year by a panel of experts, he said, simply, "The award is not mine alone. It is everyone's." That attitude explains why, when you visit Blue Water Cafe, you can reasonably expect the best—in service, in wine, in cooking, in seafood and ultimately in a fine-dining experience.

Jean-Pierre Sanchez, pastry chef

FISH

FRESHWATER AND SALTWATER FISH

THESE ARE troubled times for fisheries worldwide, but Frank Pabst is among a small but growing number of chefs around the world who see alternatives to either turning a blind eye or surrendering to wholesale panic. "Sustainability is vital," he says. "It is simple for me. The thought of what happened, or is happening, to certain species made me not want to eat them anymore. And certainly not to cook them anymore." Blue Water Cafe is wholly dedicated to exploring the best the ocean has to offer, and in the case of the Pacific Coast, that is a plentiful boatful, certainly. But the approach is always to be aware of such collateral effects of fishing as habitat damage, bycatch (other species caught incidentally in a trawl, net or dredge) and stock number fluctuations.

The Vancouver Aquarium's Ocean Wise program and Monterey Bay Aquarium's Seafood Watch program—conservation initiatives to help consumers make seafood choices that have the least environmental impact—are resources Frank uses to determine if a fish is right for Blue Water Cafe. The David Suzuki Foundation is also part of the solution, providing scientific analysis and keeping a close eye on the work that governmental agencies do in managing the fisheries. Frank discusses the issues in a matter-of-fact way, but he is very serious about sourcing fish for Blue Water Cafe. "I am looking for consistency, quality and, of course, a good price. I know our suppliers well and I know they source their catches properly. And, in the end, I am interested in exploring new flavours and new ideas and sharing these with our clients." This means guests at Blue Water Cafe can experience creative and classical treatments of species not commonly offered at all and seldom seen in a fine-dining restaurant.

Pacific Halibut are flounders available from late spring to early winter and, as such, are a substantial part of Blue Water Cafe's menu during this period. Halibut can weigh up to 200 pounds when mature and can measure over 9¾ feet in length, but the average size of halibut used at the restaurant is 30 pounds. Halibut are line-caught fish, caught in the deep waters to the west of British Columbia's island coastline. They make their way fresh to market, and to dining tables, prized for their somewhat lean flesh, which is sweet and moist if cooked properly.

Sablefish, once considered bycatch, are the new luxury fish. As Frank dryly notes, "It was called black cod, but nobody would order it. So the name was changed to sablefish." The move seemed to work, and now they even make a fairly regular appearance on the television program *Iron Chef America*. In British Columbia and Alaska, the catch is abundant and sustainable, given the policy of using only longlines or traps and pots. Individual Vessel Quotas (IVQs) mean the fishery is open year-round. Although sablefish spawn in relatively shallow waters, they migrate to the deep, usually around 4900 feet, where they mature and where harvesting takes place. Their unctuous, mild, somewhat sweet meat matches so well with a variety of treatments that it remains one of Frank's favourites, well into his second decade of using it. It has a remarkable flaking quality that makes it a chef's choice in terms of presentation and dining experience.

Salmon are the undisputed kings of Pacific Coast seafood, because of both their numbers and their rich flavour profile, the result of omega-3 fatty acids. The Salmonid family includes chinook, coho, sockeye, chum, pink and steelhead. Arctic char rounds out the group. Each of these has a

highly individualized spawning season and therefore the fisheries vary. Late spring to early autumn covers the overall spread of the fishery. Salmon range also in size, from the smallest pink salmon at 3 to 5 pounds to some of the chinook weighing in at up to 135 pounds. Salmon are anadromous, living at least a part of their lives in both salt and fresh water, and their runs are highly particular; the fish famously—and in scientific terms, mysteriously—return to spawn in the exact stream in which they were hatched, even if, as in the case of some sockeye runs, the time lapse is measured in many years.

The controversy surrounding "open" salmon farms has essentially been resolved: salmon farmers need to reinvent the wheel in order to prevent diseases such as sea lice, habitat damage due to lack of waste management and potentially irreparable harm to wild salmon runs, near which many of the farms are placed. Still, aquaculture has its merits and its place. Trout farms—generally in freshwater lakes—and arctic char farms do not have the same problems as salmon farms and are recognized by aquariums from Alaska through Vancouver to Monterey Bay for offering consumers conscientious and sustainable choices. Salmon are available all year round, in part because of relatively new fishing technology, which includes an ice-cold brine bath that freezes the fish at sea by forming an ice surface all around the whole fish while not causing any damage to the flesh itself.

Trout that remain strictly freshwater are known as rainbow trout and are considered distinct from rainbow trout that make their way to the ocean, becoming steelhead trout, which are classified as salmon. Steelhead are a prized game fish, and the commercial catch is virtually non-existent, so the trout you find at a respectable restaurant are likely to be freshwater rainbow, and farmed.

Sturgeon are prehistoric giants that can live to a hundred years or more, attain a length of 23 feet and weigh over 1650 pounds. Severely endangered in other parts of the world, the protected freshwater sturgeon are still alive and well in the Pacific Northwest, mostly at the bottom of the Fraser River. British Columbia boasts a successful sturgeon farm and, at some point in the near future, will potentially offer a New World caviar production to accompany it. For now, Blue Water Cafe sources its sturgeon from a pristine farm environment in Idaho. The meat is somewhat dense and flavourful, and it matches amazingly well with a delicate Italian dolcetto.

Tuna is a fish with several species—nearly fifty, in fact, and the fisheries they support as an ensemble are formidable. Albacore, which are stars at Blue Water Cafe, are there at all by the graces of pole fishing—not, under any circumstances, trawl or net fishing. Pole fishing is just what it sounds like: a hook and line attached to a fishing pole. This technique is most often used in sport fisheries as part of a catch-and-release program, but pole fishing is still occasionally commercially used. Albacore are among the smallest of tuna, usually around 66 pounds and rarely exceeding 3¼ feet. The tuna season runs all year, though catches are increasingly being limited, particularly for the larger varieties.

Ling cod, which are subject to the same rules of fishing methods, are a distant relative of fellow bottom-feeders the rockfish and not a relative to cod at all. Their moist, mild white meat can sustain a variety of cooking methods and accompanying sauces or preparations, so it is ideal for Blue Water Cafe. Line caught, ling cod are a completely sustainable product, available in controlled amounts throughout the year; catch limits are in place. Sport fisheries prize the larger specimens, often in the 66-pound range, found at depths of 985 feet. The norm for ling cod, though, is 22 to 33 pounds.

Pan-roasted Halibut

with Braised Lobster Mushrooms and Potato Gnocchi

SERVES 4

Gnocchi

- 1 large russet potato, about 9 oz
- 3/4 cup pastry flour
- 1 egg yolk
- 2 Tbsp olive oil

Halibut and Mushrooms

- 1 lb lobster mushrooms, cleaned under cold water with a soft brush
- 6 Tbsp olive oil
- 1 clove garlic, thinly sliced
- 1 sprig thyme
- 12 small cipollini onions, peeled and halved
- 1/3 cup white wine
- 1/2 cup chicken stock (page 184)
- 3/4 cup beurre blanc (page 188)
- 4 sprigs parsley, chiffonaded
- 1/2 lemon
- 4 halibut fillets, 5 oz each, skin removed

Orange-red lobster mushrooms are dense in texture and have a seafood-like flavour. They are available locally throughout the summer at farmer's markets and specialty food stores, as are cipollini onions. If you cannot find these ingredients, substitute pine mushrooms for the lobster mushrooms and try pearl onions or spring onions in place of the cipollini onions.

Gnocchi Preheat the oven to 350°F. Bake potato for 45 to 55 minutes until fork tender. Remove from the oven, split the potato open and allow the steam to escape for 5 minutes. Pass the potato through a ricer and measure its weight. Measure half the amount of the potato weight in pastry flour, and sift it into the potato. Add egg yolk and a good pinch of salt, then mix the ingredients together with your fingertips until a smooth ball forms. Cover the dough with a kitchen towel and allow it to rest for 15 minutes.

Lightly dust a sheet of parchment paper with flour. On a separate floured surface, roll out the dough to a long cylinder ½ inch in diameter. Cut the cylinder into 1-inch-long pieces. Place the gnocchi on the parchment paper.

Fill a large bowl with ice water. Bring a large pot of salted water to a boil on high heat. Add gnocchi and cook, stirring once or twice, until they rise to the surface and the water returns to a boil, about 1 minute. Transfer gnocchi to the ice bath and allow to cool. Pat gnocchi dry, toss with olive oil and reserve until needed.

Halibut and mushrooms Cut and discard ⅓ inch from the bottom of the mushroom stems. Cut the mushrooms into ¼-inch slices.

Heat 4 Tbsp of the olive oil in a wide pan on medium heat. Add lobster mushrooms and season with salt and pepper. Cook for 5 minutes until the oil takes on a yellowish tinge. Add garlic, thyme and cipollini onions and cook for about 2 minutes, until fragrant. Deglaze the pan with wine and cook until liquid has reduced by three-quarters, 2 to 3 minutes. Add chicken stock and cook until liquid has reduced by three-quarters, about 5 minutes. Remove thyme. Stir in beurre blanc and remove from the heat. Add parsley, then season with salt, pepper and a squeeze of lemon.

Heat 2 Tbsp of olive oil in a large sauté pan on medium-high heat. Season halibut fillets with salt and pepper, then add to the pan and sear for 3 to 4 minutes per side until both sides have a golden crust and the fish is cooked to medium or medium rare with an opaque centre.

To serve Add gnocchi to the mushroom sauce, tossing to coat. Spoon the mushrooms, onions and sauce onto the centre of each of four plates. Top the mushrooms with a fillet of halibut, then spoon a quarter of the gnocchi around the plate.

Suggested wine Try a vintage Champagne with a yeasty character and good acidity.

Grilled Halibut Tail

with Golden Raisin and Pickled Nasturtium Sauce

SERVES 4

Pickled nasturtium seeds

- 2 cups water
- 4 Tbsp pickling salt
- 2 cups plump green nasturtium seeds
- 2 cups white wine vinegar

Halibut tail

- 8 small fingerling potatoes, halved lengthwise
- 1 small head cauliflower, cut in florets
- 5 Tbsp olive oil
- 20 pearl onions, peeled
- Tail end of a halibut, 10 inches long, skin on but fin removed
- 1 Tbsp unsalted butter
- 1 Tbsp nigella seeds
- ½ cup Italian parsley, chiffonaded
- 2 cups pea tendrils
- 1 lemon, in wedges

Pickled nasturtium seeds are similar to capers. The seeds must be pickled for a month before using, and the best nasturtium seeds for pickling are those in half-ripened pods that are still green, picked as soon as the nasturtium flowers wilt and fall off. You may be able to find nasturtium seeds at farmer's markets or you can grow them yourself. If neither of these options is possible, substitute capers for the pickled nasturtium seeds. Nigella seeds are a spice with a slightly bitter taste; they are available from Asian food stores.

Pickled nasturtium seeds In a medium saucepan, bring water and salt to a boil until salt is completely dissolved. Allow to cool, then refrigerate this brine. Add nasturtium seeds and soak for 24 hours.

Sterilize a 4-cup pickling jar by submerging it in boiling water for 1 to 2 minutes. Remove from the water and allow to cool and air dry on a rack at room temperature. Drain the seeds, but do not rinse them. In a medium saucepan, bring vinegar to a boil. Pack the seeds into the pickling jar, then add hot vinegar and seal the jar tightly. Store the jar in a cool place for 1 month before using.

Halibut tail Bring a medium pot of salted water to a boil on high heat. Add potatoes and cook for about 10 minutes until tender. Remove the potatoes from the water using a slotted spoon and set them aside.

Add cauliflower to the boiling water and cook until it is done but still has some bite, about 2 minutes. Drain.

In a small sauté pan, heat 2 Tbsp of the olive oil on low heat. Add pearl onions and roast until golden and tender, about 10 minutes. Season with salt and pepper.

Preheat a grill to high. Lightly brush a plate with olive oil. Wash the halibut tail, then pat it dry with a kitchen towel and brush it with 1 Tbsp of olive oil. Season with salt and pepper and place it, white-side down, on the grill for 10 minutes. Using two large spatulas, transfer the tail from the grill onto the oiled plate. Carefully flip the tail. Clean the grill, then heat it up again on high heat. Slide the halibut tail back onto the grill, this time dark-side down. Reduce the heat to medium-high and cook for another 15 minutes.

Using the two spatulas, transfer the tail from the grill onto a large serving platter. Cover the tail with aluminum foil.

Heat 2 Tbsp of olive oil and the butter in a large sauté pan until butter starts to brown. Add cauliflower florets and fingerling potatoes and cook 5 to 10 minutes until golden. Season with salt and pepper. Toss in pearl onions, nigella seeds and parsley. Add pea tendrils and cook until wilted, about 1 minute.

Raisin-nasturtium sauce Place raisins and vermouth in a small heat-proof bowl. Microwave for 1 minute, then set aside and allow to soak for 15 minutes.

In a small saucepan, heat sugar on medium heat until it becomes a light caramel colour, about 5 minutes. Deglaze the saucepan with vinegar. Add shallots and cook for 2 minutes. Add raisins, nasturtium seeds and nasturtium leaves. Using a blender, emulsify this mixture.

To serve Remove the aluminum foil from the fish, then arrange the cauliflower mixture around the dish. Serve directly from the platter or, to serve on individual plates, discard the halibut skin, and slide the fillets off the bone. On each of four plates, place half a fillet, then spoon a quarter of the golden raisin and pickled nasturtium sauce beside it. Ladle a quarter of the cauliflower mixture alongside each serving of halibut tail. Serve with a plate of lemon wedges.

Suggested wine Opt for a wine with good aromatics and crispness on the palate, like grüner veltliner from Austria.

Raisin-nasturtium sauce

- 4 oz golden raisins
- 1/2 cup vermouth
- 3 Tbsp sugar
- 3 Tbsp white wine vinegar
- 2 shallots, minced
- 4 oz pickled nasturtium seeds, rinsed
- Handful of nasturtium leaves

Halibut Cheeks Poached in Olive Oil
with Bouillabaisse and Saffron Potatoes

facing: Grilled Halibut Tail with Golden
Raisin and Pickled Nasturtium Sauce

Halibut Cheeks Poached in Olive Oil

with Bouillabaisse and Saffron Potatoes

SERVES 4

Halibut bouillabaisse

- ½ cup olive oil
- 1 Tbsp fennel seeds
- 2 tsp saffron
- 1 tsp hot red chili flakes
- 1 small onion, minced
- 10 cloves garlic, germ removed, chopped
- 1 rib celery, minced
- 1 small leek, white and light green parts, minced
- 5 Tbsp tomato paste
- 3 large tomatoes, chopped
- 2 lbs halibut trim, skin removed
- 12 cups fish stock (page 186)
- 1 sprig thyme, 1 bay leaf, 1 sprig tarragon and 1 dried fennel stalk, tied into a bouquet garni

Halibut cheeks

- 8 halibut cheeks, sinew removed
- ½ cup salt
- 2 cups olive oil (not extra-virgin)
- 1 sprig thyme
- 1 bay leaf
- 1 Tbsp fennel seeds
- 3 cloves garlic
- 1 Tbsp thyme leaves, for garnish

Halibut bouillabaisse In a large pot, heat olive oil on medium heat. Add fennel seeds, saffron and chili flakes and cook until fragrant, about 5 minutes. Add onion, garlic, celery and leek and continue cooking for 5 minutes. Add tomato paste and chopped tomatoes, cook for another 3 minutes, then add halibut and cook for 5 more minutes. Add fish stock, bouquet garni and a pinch of salt and simmer for 30 minutes.

Remove the bouquet garni and blend the soup for 5 minutes with a hand-held blender until well emulsified. Strain the soup through a medium-mesh sieve into a clean pot, pressing hard on the solids to extract all the juices and essence. Discard the solids. Season the bouillabaisse with salt and pepper.

Halibut cheeks Cover cheeks with salt and allow to cure for 10 minutes. Wash off the salt in plenty of cold water and pat the fish dry with a kitchen towel.

In a medium pot, heat olive oil, thyme, bay leaf, fennel seeds and garlic to 200°F—check the temperature with a thermometer—and allow the flavours to infuse for 10 minutes. Add halibut cheeks, making sure all of the pieces are submerged. Cook for about 6 minutes until the cheeks are just done, adjusting the heat to keep the oil at 200°F.

Remove the cheeks from the oil and allow to drain on paper towels. Strain the oil and reserve it for future use.

Saffron potatoes In a large pot, heat olive oil on medium heat. Add onion, garlic, chili flakes, thyme, bay leaf, star anise and saffron and sweat until fragrant, about 5 minutes. Add water and simmer for 10 minutes. Strain the liquid through a medium-mesh sieve into a clean pot, discarding the solids, and season with salt and pepper. Add potato slices and cook slowly on low heat for 3 to 5 minutes until potatoes are done. Remove the pot from the heat and allow potatoes to cool in the saffron broth to absorb all the flavours. Set aside until needed.

Saffron potatoes

- 3 Tbsp olive oil
- ½ onion, minced
- 2 cloves garlic, chopped
- 1 tsp hot red chili flakes
- 1 sprig thyme
- 1 bay leaf
- 1 pod star anise
- Pinch of saffron
- 2 cups water
- 8 fingerling potatoes, sliced on a mandolin then rinsed in cold water

Rouille

- 3 cloves garlic, germ removed
- 2 egg yolks
- 1 cup olive oil
- Pinch of cayenne pepper
- 1 tsp saffron threads
- 1 Tbsp halibut bouillabaisse

Garlic croutons

- 2 Tbsp olive oil
- 12 thin slices of baguette
- 2 cloves garlic

Rouille In a mortar, crush garlic with a pinch of salt to a fine paste. Transfer the paste to a small bowl. Whisk in egg yolks, then add olive oil in a thin stream, whisking constantly, to obtain an aioli. In a small bowl, stir cayenne and saffron into the bouillabaisse, then stir this mixture into the aioli.

Garlic croutons Heat olive oil in a sauté pan on medium heat. Add bread slices and fry until golden brown on both sides, 3 to 4 minutes. Rub each slice on one side with a clove of garlic.

To serve Arrange the saffron potatoes in the centre of four bowls and top with two halibut cheeks. Serve the bouillabaisse in a soup tureen on the side and pass around small bowls containing the rouille and the croutons. Guests can add the bouillabaisse to their bowls along with croutons, rouille and a pinch of thyme leaves.

Suggested wine A wine high in minerality would work well with this dish—Chablis would be a good start.

Sablefish

Caramelized with Soy and Sake

SERVES 4

Tamarind is a tart fruit that is used in chutneys and pickles, and is often ground to obtain a paste. It is available in many Asian food stores. This recipe also calls for mirin, a sweet cooking wine. Find it at an Asian supermarket.

Soy-sake marinade In a small saucepan, bring all ingredients to a boil on high heat. Reduce the heat to medium-high and simmer until sugar is dissolved and alcohol has evaporated, about 2 minutes. Remove from the heat, allow the mixture to cool, then refrigerate until well chilled.

Orange-tamarind sauce In a large saucepan, heat olive oil on medium heat. Add carrot, celery, onion, garlic, jalapeño and ginger and sweat for 5 to 10 minutes until fragrant. Add mustard seeds, peppercorns, thyme, bay leaf, vinegar, orange juice, tamarind paste and chicken stock and cook until liquid has reduced by two-thirds, 20 to 30 minutes. Strain the sauce through a fine-mesh sieve into a clean bowl, then season with salt and pepper. Add kumquats. Will keep refrigerated in an airtight container for up to 7 days.

Caramelized sablefish Combine sablefish and soy-sake marinade in a resealable plastic zip-top bag and refrigerate overnight.

Heat a medium pot of salted water to a boil. Add beans and blanch for 2 to 3 minutes. Transfer the beans to a bowl and toss in butter. Season with salt and pepper.

Heat canola oil in a deep fryer or a deep pot to 300°F. Mix flour and cayenne in a bowl. Toss shallot slices in this seasoned flour to dredge, then fry them in the oil until golden and crisp, about 30 seconds. Remove the shallot slices from the oil and allow to drain on paper towels.

Remove the sablefish fillets from the refrigerator and allow them to warm to room temperature.

Turn the broiler on. Transfer the sablefish, skin-side down, to a cast-iron pan and place it on the lowest rack under the broiler for 5 to 10 minutes until deeply caramelized. (The cooking time will depend upon the thickness of the fillets.)

To serve Arrange a quarter of the green beans in the centre of each of four plates. Using a metal spatula, lift each fillet from its skin and place the fish on the beans. Sprinkle each dish with a quarter of the fried shallots and finish with a quarter of the orange-tamarind sauce and some orange zest.

Suggested wine A pinot noir that shows good acid and fruit, such as one from Dundee Hills in Oregon.

Soy-sake marinade

- 1/2 cup sake
- 1/2 cup water
- 1/2 cup soy sauce
- 1 Tbsp brown sugar
- 1 Tbsp mirin

Orange-tamarind sauce

- 3 Tbsp olive oil
- 1 small carrot, sliced
- 1 rib celery, sliced
- 1/2 onion, sliced
- 3 cloves garlic, sliced
- 1/4 jalapeño pepper, sliced
- 1-inch piece of ginger, sliced
- 1 tsp mustard seeds
- 1 tsp black peppercorns
- 1 sprig thyme
- 1 bay leaf
- 1/4 cup balsamic vinegar
- 1/4 cup concentrated orange juice
- 2 Tbsp tamarind paste
- 4 cups chicken stock (page 184)
- 8 kumquats, sliced and seeded
- Zest of 1/4 orange, julienned, for garnish

Caramelized sablefish

- 4 sablefish fillets, 6 oz each, skin on
- 1 1/2 cups soy-sake marinade
- 10 oz green beans
- 2 Tbsp unsalted butter
- 2 cups canola oil, for deep-frying
- 4 Tbsp flour
- Pinch of cayenne pepper
- 4 shallots, thinly sliced on a mandolin

Sablefish Collars

with Nori Seaweed and Potato Scales

SERVES 4

Sablefish collars

- 1 egg white
- 3 sheets nori seaweed
- 1/4 cup instant potato flakes
- 12 sablefish collars
- 1/4 cup potato starch
- 1 cup canola oil
- 7 oz small mizuna leaves

Remoulade

- 1/3 cup Japanese mayonnaise
- 1 Tbsp pickled ginger, chopped
- 1 tsp grated fresh ginger
- 1 Tbsp rice vinegar
- 1 Tbsp yuzu juice
- 2 green onions, thinly sliced
- 1 Tbsp black sesame seeds
- 1 sprig parsley, chopped (about 1 Tbsp)

Sesame vinaigrette

- 3 Tbsp dark sesame oil
- 3 Tbsp canola oil
- 2 Tbsp tamari
- 3 Tbsp rice vinegar
- 1 Tbsp honey
- 1 Tbsp black sesame seeds
- 1 Tbsp white sesame seeds, toasted
- 3 green onions, minced

The collar of the sablefish is the area between the head and the body, and the meat under the collar is succulent and resembles halibut cheeks in texture. To make this dish, you will need nori, the familiar seaweed used to roll maki sushi, sold in dried sheets; yuzu juice, the juice from a tart citrus fruit originating in East Asia and frequently used in Japanese cuisine; tamari, a dark, rich variety of soy sauce; Japanese mayonnaise, a thinner mayonnaise made with rice vinegar, and mizuna, Japanese mustard greens. All of these ingredients are available at most Asian supermarkets and are becoming more and more common in mainstream grocery stores.

Sablefish collars In a small bowl, gently whip egg white with a pinch of salt.

Shred nori sheets into a clean coffee grinder and coarsely grind the seaweed, then mix with potato flakes in a shallow dish.

Remove any sinew from the sablefish collar meat, then toss it in potato starch. Shake off excess starch and toss the fish in the egg white. Allow excess egg white to drip off, then toss the fish in the nori–potato flake mixture to coat.

Heat canola oil in a wide pan to 350°F (use a deep-fat thermometer to check the temperature). Add crusted sablefish and fry for 1 minute on each side. Remove the fish from the oil and drain on paper towels. Season with salt and pepper.

Remoulade In a small bowl, mix together all of the ingredients and season with salt and pepper.

Sesame vinaigrette In a small bowl, whisk together all of the ingredients until well blended.

To serve In a medium bowl, toss mizuna greens with six tablespoons of the sesame vinaigrette and divide equally on one side of four plates. Spoon two to three tablespoons of the remoulade on the other side of the plate, then top with three sablefish collars per serving.

Suggested wine Go for a stronger white like a Napa Valley chardonnay. If you prefer red, try a Cru Beaujolais.

Smoked Black Cod

with Beluga Lentils, Horseradish Froth and Beet Straw

SERVES 4

Cod and lentils

- 1 cup organic black beluga lentils, washed
- 1 small carrot, peeled
- 1 rib celery
- 2 cloves garlic
- 2-inch piece of leek
- 1 small Roma tomato
- 1 sprig thyme
- 1 bay leaf
- 1 slice smoked bacon
- 2½ cups chicken stock, or more (page 184)
- 2 Tbsp canola oil
- 4 smoked black cod fillets (not dyed), 5 oz each, skin and bones removed
- 2 Tbsp balsamic vinegar
- 3 Tbsp unsalted butter
- ½ cup Italian parsley, chiffonaded
- ½ lemon
- Handful of garnet beet shoots or sprigs chervil, for garnish

Horseradish froth

- ½ cup white wine sauce (page 188)
- 2 Tbsp freshly grated horseradish
- ½ lemon
- ¼ tsp soy lecithin

Beet straw

- 4 cups canola oil, for deep-frying
- 1 large red beet, peeled and finely julienned to pieces 2 inches long

For this recipe, buy smoked sablefish, or black cod, from your fishmonger rather than preparing your own. Beluga lentils are very small black lentils that look like large caviar and cook quickly, so there is no need to soak them overnight. To make the horseradish froth, you will need soy lecithin, a stabilizing ingredient. It is available at most specialty food stores.

Cod and lentils In a large pot, combine lentils, carrot, celery, garlic, leek, tomato, thyme, bay leaf, bacon and chicken stock and cook on medium heat for 20 to 30 minutes until lentils are done but still have some bite and most of the liquid has been absorbed. (If the chicken stock is fully absorbed before the lentils are cooked, add more stock, 2 oz at a time, and continue to cook until the lentils are done.) Season with salt and pepper and set aside.

In a large sauté pan, heat canola oil on high heat. Carefully add smoked black cod fillets. (Since smoked black cod is usually cured before the smoking process, it often does not need to be seasoned before cooking.) Reduce the heat to medium and cook for 3 to 5 minutes per side, depending on the thickness of the fillets, until both sides are golden brown and the fish is cooked. Remove the fillets from the pan and place them on a paper towel to absorb excess oil.

Remove and discard carrot, celery, garlic, leek, tomato, thyme, bay leaf and bacon from the lentils. Stir in vinegar, butter and parsley. Season with salt, pepper and a squeeze of lemon juice.

Horseradish froth In a small saucepan, bring all of the ingredients to a simmer on low heat. Season with salt and pepper and, using a handheld blender, froth the mixture for 2 minutes until plenty of small bubbles develop and the sauce doubles in volume. If it does not froth as desired, add a small amount of water to thin out the sauce and try frothing again.

Beet straw Preheat the oven to 175°F.

In a deep fryer or a deep pot, heat canola oil to 275°F. Add beet threads and fry them for about 60 seconds until they start to become crispy but still have their bright colour. Remove them from the oil and allow them to drain on several layers of paper towel.

Transfer the beet threads to a baking sheet. Place them in the oven and allow them to dry out further for 5 to 10 minutes until they are crispy.

To serve On each of four large plates, spoon a quarter of the lentils. Arrange a smoked black cod fillet on top. Spoon a quarter of the horseradish froth around the dish and sprinkle with a quarter of the red beet straw. Garnish with garnet beet shoots or chervil sprigs.

Suggested wine If you're adventurous, try this dish with an aged Bandol from southern France.

Citrus-cured Sockeye Salmon

with White Asparagus and Poached Hen's Eggs

SERVES 4

Lemon vinegar is available at specialty food stores, but if you cannot find it, use half lemon juice and half champagne vinegar instead. The salmon in this recipe is cured over three days.

Honey mustard Mix together all ingredients in a small bowl until well blended.

Cured salmon Line a dish, just big enough for the salmon, with plastic wrap.

Mix together sea salt, sugar, peppercorns, coriander seeds, dill, and orange, lemon and lime zests. Spread half of this mixture on the plastic wrap, place the salmon fillet, skin-side up, on top, and cover the fillet with the rest of the salt mixture. Add orange, lemon and lime juices, then wrap the plastic tightly around the fillet. Place a 2-lb weight on top and refrigerate for 24 hours.

Rinse the salmon under running water to remove the marinade, pat it dry and refrigerate, uncovered on a plate, overnight.

Spread honey mustard evenly on the salmon fillet, cover with chopped herbs, wrap tightly in plastic wrap and refrigerate once again overnight.

Bring a medium pot of salted water to a boil on high heat. Stir in a pinch of sugar, then add asparagus and cook for 9 minutes. Remove the asparagus from the pot and cut each spear into four pieces.

In a large pot, combine the 8 cups of water and the vinegar, then bring this mixture to a simmer on low heat. Crack an egg into the liquid and poach for 3 to 4 minutes. Repeat until all eggs are poached.

Honey-mustard vinaigrette Whisk together all ingredients, along with a pinch of salt and pepper, in a small bowl until well emulsified.

To serve Reserve four pieces of asparagus. Combine the remaining asparagus and mizuna greens in a bowl. Reserve two tablespoons of vinaigrette for the garnish. Add the remaining vinaigrette to the asparagus and mizuna greens, tossing gently to coat.

With a long, thin-bladed knife, cut the cured salmon into very thin slices. Remove the skin, then cut the flesh into pieces 3 to 5 inches long.

Arrange a quarter of the asparagus and mizuna greens in the centre of each of four plates. Place two slices of the citrus-cured salmon on top and top the salmon with a poached egg. Sprinkle the egg with a little coarse sea salt. Finish the dish with a drizzle of vinaigrette and a piece of asparagus.

Suggested wine A crisp riesling from Marlborough, New Zealand.

Honey mustard

3 Tbsp grainy mustard
2 Tbsp Dijon mustard
2 Tbsp wildflower honey

Cured salmon

½ cup coarse sea salt
¼ cup sugar + a pinch for cooking asparagus
1 Tbsp white peppercorns
1 Tbsp coriander seeds
1 bunch dill, chopped
Juice and zest of 3 oranges
Juice and zest of 2 lemons
Juice and zest of 2 limes
1 side of sockeye salmon, about 3 ¼ lbs, skin on, pin bones removed
5 Tbsp honey mustard
4 oz finely chopped mixed fresh herbs, such as chervil, lemon balm, dill, chives and Italian parsley (about ½ cup)
8 large spears white asparagus, peeled
8 cups cold water
½ cup white vinegar
4 organic eggs
1 bunch small mizuna greens

Honey-mustard vinaigrette

⅓ cup extra-virgin olive oil
2 Tbsp organic lemon vinegar
2 Tbsp honey mustard

Chum Salmon Wrapped in Swiss Chard

with Pacific Oysters and Saffron Sauce

SERVES 4

- 1 chum salmon fillet, 7 oz, diced
- 7 oz whipping cream (slightly less than 1 cup)
- 1/2 lemon
- 12 small Pacific oysters
- 1 bunch Swiss chard
- 1 cup fish stock (page 186)
- 1/2 cup dry white wine
- Pinch of espelette pepper
- Pinch of saffron
- 6 Tbsp unsalted butter, cold
- 2 Tbsp olive oil
- 6 cipollini onions, thinly sliced
- 1 clove garlic, crushed
- 1 sprig thyme
- 2 to 4 sprigs chervil, for garnish

Espelette pepper is a red pepper cultivated in France. It is available at specialty food stores.

Place a medium bowl and the bowl of a food processor in the refrigerator until well chilled, about 10 minutes.

Place the salmon into the chilled bowl of the food processor, then process for 1 minute, add ¼ cup of the cream and mix for another 30 seconds. Pass this mixture through a fine-mesh sieve into the chilled bowl, then fold in ¼ cup of the cream. Whip the remaining cream to soft peaks and fold it into the salmon mousse, then season with salt and a squeeze of lemon juice.

Shuck the oysters, reserving all of the oyster liquor and ensuring that all small pieces of shell have been removed from the meat. Dry the oysters on a kitchen towel.

Fill a large bowl with ice water. Cut the Swiss chard leaves off their stems. Using a small knife, pull off the stringy parts of the stems. Thinly slice the stems. Bring a small pot of salted water to a boil on high heat. Add chard leaves and blanch for 30 seconds, plunge them into the ice bath to refresh, then dry them on a kitchen towel. Next, blanch the stems for 1 minute, then refresh them in the ice bath.

Cut the chard leaves into twelve pieces about 4 inches square and lay them out on a cutting board. Keep the smaller leaf trimmings to the side.

Wrap each oyster with one of the smaller pieces of chard leaf. Spread 1 heaped tablespoon of the salmon mousse into the centre of each of the bigger squares, top with a wrapped oyster, then add another dollop of mousse on top. Fold the bottom half of the chard leaf over the filling, tuck in the sides and fold the top of the chard over the bottom like an envelope to make a little package.

In a large, shallow pan, bring fish stock to a simmer on medium heat and place all the Swiss chard packages in a single layer into the liquid. Cover the pan and poach the packages for 4 to 5 minutes. Remove the packages from the pan and allow them to drain on a kitchen towel.

To the poaching liquid, add the reserved oyster liquor, wine, espelette pepper and saffron and heat until liquid has reduced by two-thirds, about 15 minutes. Whisk in chilled butter. Season to taste with salt and pepper.

In a medium sauté pan, heat olive oil on medium-low heat. Add cipollini onions, Swiss chard stems, garlic and thyme and cook until vegetables are tender but not browned, about 10 minutes. Season with salt and a squeeze of lemon juice. Remove and discard the garlic and thyme.

To serve In the centre of each of four plates, spoon a quarter of the onions and chard stems. Top with three salmon-oyster packages and spoon saffron sauce around the dish. Garnish with chervil sprigs.

Suggested wine Try a wine with a mineral aroma and stone-fruit notes, such as roussanne from Santa Barbara County.

Wild Spring Salmon

with Braised Fennel, Vanilla and Green Olives

SERVES 4

Braised fennel Preheat the oven to 375°F. Heat olive oil in a large ovenproof sauté pan on medium heat. Add fennel, garlic, shallots, thyme and bay leaf and sauté for about 5 minutes until fragrant. Season with salt and pepper.

Deglaze the pan with wine and chicken stock. Bring the mixture to a boil and stir in olives and Roma tomatoes. Cover the pan with aluminum foil and braise in the oven for about 20 minutes until vegetables are just tender. Use a slotted spoon to transfer fennel and olives to a second ovenproof pan and set them aside.

Add fennel seeds and vanilla bean, both seeds and pod, to the remaining liquid and cook it on medium-high heat until it has reduced by half, about 12 minutes.

Discard the vanilla pod. Purée the braising mixture in a blender, then pass the sauce through a fine-mesh sieve into a clean bowl. Season with lemon juice, salt and pepper. Reduce the oven temperature to 200°F.

Add parsley and grape tomatoes to the fennel and olives. Pour the sauce over the fennel mixture, toss well to combine, and keep warm in the oven.

Salmon Heat a sauté pan over high heat. Season fish with salt and pepper, then add olive oil to the pan. Reduce the heat to medium, add the salmon and sear for 2 minutes on each side.

To serve Place three pieces of fennel in each of four large, shallow bowls. Add a quarter of the sauce, then top with a fillet of salmon and finish with a drizzle of olive oil.

Suggested wine Pinot blanc from B.C. or Alsace.

Braised fennel

- 2 Tbsp olive oil
- 2 bulbs fennel, trimmed and cut in 6 pieces each
- 4 cloves garlic, chopped
- 3 large shallots, chopped
- 2 sprigs fresh thyme
- 1 bay leaf
- 1 cup dry, crisp chardonnay
- 3 cups chicken stock (page 184)
- 24 small organic green olives, pitted
- 2 Roma tomatoes, roughly chopped
- 1 tsp fennel seeds
- 1/2 vanilla bean, seeds scraped but pod reserved
- Juice of 1/2 lemon
- 2 Tbsp chopped parsley
- 12 grape tomatoes, halved

Salmon

- 4 fresh, wild spring salmon fillets, 5 oz each, skin removed
- 2 Tbsp olive oil, for searing salmon
- Drizzle of extra-virgin olive oil, for garnish

Arctic Char

with Mountain Caviar, Kohlrabi, Broccolini and Japanese Peppercress

SERVES 4

- 3 kohlrabi, peeled and cut in 1/2-inch dice
- 4 stalks broccolini
- 4 arctic char fillets, 5 oz each, skin on
- 2 Tbsp olive oil
- 1/2 cup beurre blanc (page 188)
- 2 Tbsp mountain caviar (tonburi)
- 1/2 lemon
- Handful of Japanese peppercress (benitade), for garnish

Mountain caviar is also known as tonburi *and is the seed of a Japanese cypress tree. It is usually sold preserved in glass jars and can be found in specialty Japanese food stores, where you can also find* benitade, *or Japanese peppercress, which are tiny red sprouts with a slightly peppery taste. If you cannot find Japanese peppercress, substitute regular peppercress or just omit the garnish.*

Bring a small pot of salted water to a boil. Add kohlrabi and cook until tender, about 2 minutes. Remove the kohlrabi with a slotted spoon and set aside. Add broccolini to the salted water and cook for 30 seconds. Drain and set aside.

Season char fillets with salt and pepper. In a medium sauté pan, heat olive oil on medium-high heat. Add char, skin-side down, and cook until skin becomes crispy and golden, about 3 minutes. Turn the char and cook for 1 minute or less until the fish is done.

Warm beurre blanc in a small saucepan on medium heat—do not boil. Add kohlrabi and mountain caviar. Season with a squeeze of lemon juice and salt.

To serve In the centre of four plates, spoon a quarter of the kohlrabi, mountain caviar and beurre blanc. Top with a char fillet, and garnish with a stalk of broccolini and a quarter of the peppercress.

Suggested wine A Savennières from the Loire Valley would offer the right amount of lively acidity.

Poached Arctic Char

with Braised Leeks and Wakame Seaweed

SERVES 4

Wakame is a type of kelp that is reminiscent of spinach and is commonly used in such popular Japanese dishes as miso soup and sunomono salad. Fresh wakame is preserved in salt and should be rinsed before using; look for it in specialty Japanese food stores.

Shuck oysters and reserve them in their liquor.

Season the char fillets with salt and pepper. Slice half of the lemon to yield four thin slices. Lay lemon slices in a large sauté pan and top with char fillets. Add Noilly Prat and vegetable stock, and cover the pan. Poach char on medium heat for 4 minutes.

Remove char fillets from the pan and set them aside. Discard the lemon slices. Heat poaching liquid, shallot and oyster liquor on medium heat until liquid has reduced by half, about 5 minutes. Add white wine sauce and 2 raw oysters, then transfer to a blender and purée for 30 seconds. Strain this mixture through a fine-mesh sieve into a small saucepan and season with salt and pepper and a squeeze of lemon juice. Add the remainng oysters and keep warm on low heat.

In a small covered pan, combine butter, water, leeks, onions and a pinch of salt and cook for about 4 minutes on medium heat until all liquid has evaporated and leeks are tender. Toss in the wakame and remove from the heat.

To serve Heap a quarter of the braised leek and seaweed mix on one side of each of four plates. Remove the crispy skin from each fish fillet and arrange one piece on each mound of braised leeks. Place a fillet of poached char beside the leeks and garnish it with a quarter of the chives. Spoon the oyster sauce around the plate and garnish the dish with chervil sprigs.

Suggested wine With this dish, subtlety is key, so try a nice pinot gris from Oregon.

- 10 medium Pacific oysters
- 4 arctic char fillets, 5 oz each, skin on
- 1 lemon, halved
- 1/2 cup Noilly Prat
- 1 cup vegetable stock (page 184)
- 1 shallot, sliced
- 1/2 cup white wine sauce (page 188)
- 1 Tbsp unsalted butter
- 2 Tbsp water
- 2 to 3 leeks, white part only, thinly sliced and thoroughly rinsed
- 1 white onion, quartered and thinly sliced
- 1 oz fresh wakame seaweed, rinsed, squeezed dry and cut in 1-inch pieces
- 1 tsp minced chives
- Several sprigs chervil, for garnish

Arctic Char

with Sorrel Sauce and Crab-stuffed Butter Lettuce

SERVES 4

- 2 heads butter lettuce, each with a dense yellow centre
- 3 Tbsp olive oil
- 2 shallots, diced
- 1 sprig thyme
- 1/4 cup chicken stock (page 184)
- 1/3 cup white wine
- 1/3 cup butter
- 1 1/4 oz fresh Dungeness crab meat
- 1 Tbsp mayonnaise
- Pinch of espelette pepper
- 1/2 lemon
- 4 arctic char fillets, 5 oz each, skin on
- 4 sorrel leaves

Remove the outer leaves from the lettuce. Cut the heads in half and check for fruit flies or dirt. Wash the lettuce in salted water and dry on a kitchen towel.

Heat 1 Tbsp of the olive oil in a large sauté pan on medium heat. Add shallots and thyme and sweat until fragrant, about 2 minutes. Add butter lettuce, cut-side down, and add chicken stock. Season with salt and pepper and cook, covered, for 2 minutes until butter lettuce has completely collapsed. Remove the lettuce from the pan, pressing it gently to extract any liquid. Dry the lettuce on a kitchen towel and allow it to cool in the refrigerator. Discard the thyme.

Add wine to the cooking juices from the lettuce and heat on medium heat until liquid has reduced by two-thirds, 3 to 5 minutes. Whisk in butter. Strain this sauce through a fine-mesh sieve into a saucepan.

Pick through crab meat and remove any small pieces of shell. Mix the crab meat with mayonnaise. Season with espelette pepper, salt and a squeeze of lemon juice. Divide this mixture into four portions.

Take the butter lettuce out of the refrigerator. Place a portion of crab meat inside each lettuce half and roll up the lettuce into a log, pressing gently to maintain the shape. Place the stuffed lettuce into the butter sauce and reheat on medium heat.

Season char with salt and pepper. Heat 2 Tbsp of olive oil in a large sauté pan over medium-high heat. Add char, skin-side down, and cook until skin becomes crispy and golden, about 3 minutes. Turn the char fillets and cook for 1 minute or less until they are done.

To serve On each of four plates, place a crab-stuffed lettuce wrap beside a fillet of char. Mix the butter sauce with the sorrel in a blender and season with lemon juice and salt. Spoon a quarter of the sauce over each plate.

Suggested wine Try a good Burgundian white, like a Chassagne Montrachet from the 2002 or 2004 vintage.

Whole Trout

Baked with Wakame Seaweed in a Salt Crust

SERVES 4

Whisk egg whites to a soft foam, then incorporate salt, peppercorns and the leaves from half of the thyme.

Brush each trout with 1 Tbsp of the olive oil, then stuff each fish with a quarter of the remaining thyme sprigs.

Preheat the oven to 425°F. Line a baking sheet with parchment paper. Divide the salt into eight portions. Heap four separate portions of salt on the baking sheet as bases for the trout. Arrange an eighth of the wakame in the centre of each base. Place a trout on each base, then top with the rest of the seaweed and cover with the remaining salt. Bake for 15 to 20 minutes. Check the doneness by inserting a long metal skewer through the salt crust into the middle of the fish and leaving it there for 20 seconds. If the tip of the skewer feels hot on your lips, the fish is done. If not, bake another 5 minutes.

To serve Crack the crust carefully with the back of a chef's knife. Remove and discard salt pieces and wakame from the fish and carefully transfer each trout onto a plate. Drizzle each serving with one tablespoon of extra-virgin olive oil and serve with a wedge of fresh lemon.

Suggested wine This dish demands a wine that shows exotic fruit. Try a sauvignon blanc from either the Sonoma Valley or Marlborough.

- 10 egg whites
- 4 Tbsp pink peppercorns
- 1 bunch fresh thyme
- 8 Tbsp extra-virgin olive oil
- 4 whole trout, 1 lb each, cleaned, gutted and scaled
- 3 lbs kosher salt
- 2 oz fresh wakame seaweed
- 1 lemon, in wedges

Trout

with Chanterelle Mushrooms, Baby Leeks, Fava Beans and Potato Cream

SERVES 4

- 6 baby leeks, in 1-inch pieces
- 1 cup fava beans in their pods
- 1 cup grape tomatoes
- 3 Tbsp olive oil
- 1 yellow-flesh potato, peeled (such as Yukon Gold)
- 1/4 cup table cream (18% milk fat)
- 6 Tbsp unsalted butter
- 1/2 lemon
- 11 oz fresh small chanterelle mushrooms, cleaned
- 1 shallot, minced
- 1/2 cup Italian parsley leaves, chiffonaded
- 8 trout fillets, 3 oz each, skin on

Baby leeks are small leeks with fewer green leaves and a sweeter flavour than regular leeks. They are usually available from spring through mid-summer.

Bring a medium pot of salted water to a boil on high heat. Add leeks and fava beans and blanch for 30 seconds. Shell the fava beans and discard the pods. Set aside.

Preheat the oven to 250°F. Toss tomatoes in a baking dish with 1 Tbsp of the olive oil, then season with salt and freshly ground pepper. Bake for 1 hour. Set aside.

Place potato in a medium pot of salted water and bring to a boil. Cook until the potato is done but not mushy, 20 to 25 minutes. Remove from water and allow it to rest for 5 minutes.

In a small saucepan, heat cream and 4 Tbsp of the butter to a simmer on medium heat. Pass the potato through a ricer into the cream mixture. Season with salt and a squeeze of lemon juice, then strain this potato cream through a fine-mesh sieve. Discard any solids.

Cut the bottoms off of the chanterelle stems. Cut larger chanterelles in half. Heat a large sauté pan with 1 Tbsp of the olive oil and 1 Tbsp of the butter on high heat until the butter begins to brown and smell nutty. Add chanterelle mushrooms and season with salt and pepper. Cook for 2 minutes, then add shallot and baby leeks. Cook for another 2 minutes, then toss in fava beans, tomatoes and parsley.

Heat the remaining 1 Tbsp of olive oil and 1 Tbsp of butter in another sauté pan on high heat until the butter begins to brown and smell nutty. Season the trout fillets with salt and pepper and place them skin-side down in the pan. Cook until the skin is crispy brown and the flesh side appears to be 80 per cent cooked, 2 to 3 minutes. Turn the fillets, baste them with a couple of spoons of the cooking fat and remove them from the pan. (The basting and the residual heat from the pan will continue to cook the fish.)

To serve Place a large spoonful of the potato cream in the centre of each of four warm plates. Top with two trout fillets and garnish with a quarter of the chanterelle mixture.

Suggested wine Try an oak-aged sémillon or White Rhône to act against the mushrooms.

Papillote of Trout

with Dungeness Crab and Riesling

SERVES 4

Herbed bread crumbs

- 1/2 cup Italian parsley leaves, chopped
- 1/4 cup panko (Japanese bread crumbs)
- Zest of 1 lemon
- 1 clove garlic, finely chopped
- 2 Tbsp olive oil

Papillote of trout

- 4 Tbsp olive oil
- 1 carrot, julienned
- 1 rib celery, julienned
- 1 leek, white and light green parts only, julienned
- 4 1/4 oz Dungeness crab meat, picked over to remove small shell pieces
- Handful of Italian parsley leaves, chiffonaded (about 1/2 cup)
- Pinch of espelette pepper
- 1/2 lemon + 1 lemon, quartered
- 1/4 cup unsalted butter
- 2 shallots, minced
- 8 trout fillets, 3 oz each, skin on
- 2/3 cup kabinett riesling
- 1/3 cup Noilly Prat

For this recipe you will need panko—light Japanese bread crumbs—which are available at Asian supermarkets.

Herbed bread crumbs Preheat the oven to 300°F. In a food processor, blend parsley leaves with panko until the bread crumbs become green, then mix in lemon zest, garlic, olive oil and a pinch of salt. Spread this mixture on a baking sheet and bake for 10 minutes until crispy but still green.

Papillote of trout Heat 2 Tbsp of olive oil in a medium sauté pan on medium heat. Add carrot, celery and leek and sauté until vegetables are cooked but still have some crunch, about 1 minute. Season with salt and pepper. In a medium bowl, combine crab meat, 2 Tbsp of olive oil and parsley. Season with espelette pepper, salt and a squeeze of lemon juice.

Cut out four sheets of parchment paper, each 18 by 12 inches. Crease each sheet along the middle lengthwise to create two halves, each 9 by 12 inches. Place a quarter of the butter on one half of each sheet. Place a quarter of the shallots and cooked vegetables on top of the butter.

Season trout fillets with salt and pepper. Place four fillets, skin-side down, on a plate and top with a quarter of the crab mixture. Cover the crab with the remaining trout fillets, skin-side up. Place the stuffed trouts on top of the cooked vegetables and fold the other half of the parchment papers over the fish.

Mix riesling with Noilly Prat. Close the edges of the parchment packages by making 1- to 2-inch folds around the perimeter. Before completely sealing the packages, add a quarter of the riesling–Noilly Prat mixture to each pouch.

Preheat the oven to 400°F. Place the papillotes on a baking sheet and bake for 12 to 15 minutes.

To serve Place each papillote on a plate. Open the papillotes with scissors (being careful of the escaping steam), then sprinkle each with a spoonful of the herbed bread crumbs and serve with a wedge of lemon.

Suggested wine Try a lighter chardonnay from B.C. or an unoaked chardonnay from California.

Grilled Sturgeon

with Wheat Berries, Celery Hearts and Peppery Greens

SERVES 4

- 4 oz wheat berries (about 1/4 cup)
- 1 cup chicken stock (page 184)
- 1 small onion, finely diced
- 1 bay leaf
- 1 carrot, finely diced
- 2/3 cup + 2 Tbsp extra-virgin olive oil
- 10 yellow ribs celery, from the heart of the stalk, in 1-inch pieces
- 4 sturgeon fillets, 5 oz each, skin removed
- 2 Tbsp aged sherry vinegar
- 1 Tbsp aged red wine vinegar
- 1 tsp Dijon mustard
- Pinch of sugar
- 1 oz chopped mixed herbs, such as chervil, Italian parsley and chives (about 2 Tbsp)
- 1 Tbsp capers, rinsed
- 4 oz of mixed peppery greens, such as arugula, watercress, peppercress, mizuna or nasturtium flowers

Wash wheat berries under running water, then soak them in a bowl of cold water overnight. Rinse them again, then transfer them to a medium pot. Add chicken stock, onion, bay leaf and a pinch of salt and cook on low heat for 1 hour. Add carrot for the last 5 minutes of cooking. The chicken stock should be fully absorbed by the time the wheat berries are done. Remove the bay leaf and stir in 2 Tbsp of olive oil to prevent the grains from clumping.

Bring a small pot of salted water to a boil. Add celery hearts and cook for 3 minutes. Drain.

Preheat a grill to medium-high. Season sturgeon with salt and pepper, then grill fillets on both sides to medium doneness—depending on the thickness of the fillets, the grilling time should be between 5 and 10 minutes.

Make a vinaigrette by whisking together the remaining ⅔ cup of olive oil, sherry and red wine vinegars and mustard in a bowl. Season with sugar, salt and pepper and add chopped herbs.

Toss the cooked wheat berries with the celery, capers and half of the vinaigrette. Season with salt and pepper. Toss the peppery greens with the remaining vinaigrette and a pinch of salt.

To serve Divide the wheat berry salad among four plates and top with grilled sturgeon. Garnish with the peppery greens.

Suggested wine Try a perfumed albariño from Rías Baixas, Spain.

Sturgeon

with Pumpernickel Crust, Cauliflower Purée and Red Beets

SERVES 4

- 2 slices pumpernickel bread
- 4 Tbsp dry bread crumbs
- 4 Tbsp salted butter, softened at room temperature
- 1/4 head cauliflower, cut in florets
- 6 Tbsp unsalted butter
- 1 small onion, diced
- 1 1/4 cups whipping cream
- 1 bunch baby beets, greens cut off, leaving 1 inch of stem
- 1 cup fish stock (page 186)
- 1 cup pinot noir
- 1 sprig thyme
- Dash of aged red wine vinegar
- 3 shallots, thinly sliced
- 4 sturgeon fillets, 5 oz each, skin removed
- 2 Tbsp olive oil

Pulse pumpernickel in a food processor until it resembles fine crumbs. Transfer to a medium bowl. Add bread crumbs and salted butter and mix to combine. Spread a ⅛-inch-thick layer of this mixture inside a large resealable plastic zip-top bag and place it in the refrigerator until the butter hardens again, about 10 minutes.

Bring a large pot of salted water to a boil on high heat. Add cauliflower florets and cook for 3 minutes until well done but not mushy. Drain.

In a medium sauté pan, heat 2 Tbsp of the unsalted butter on medium heat. Add onion and cook until soft, about 3 minutes, then add cauliflower and cream and boil for 1 minute. Purée this mixture in a blender, then season with salt and pepper.

Rinse beets. Bring a large pot of water to a boil, then add beets and cook for 5 to 10 minutes until tender. Scrub the skin off the beets with a washcloth and cut each beet in half.

In a small saucepan, combine fish stock, pinot noir, thyme, vinegar and shallots. Heat on medium heat until liquid has reduced to 5 Tbsp, about 10 minutes. Slowly whisk in the remaining 4 Tbsp of unsalted butter. Strain the sauce, return it to the saucepan, and season with salt and pepper. Add beets to the sauce and keep them warm on low heat.

Preheat the oven to 400°F. Cut the pumpernickel crust into four pieces the same size as the sturgeon fillets. Season the sturgeon, then top each fillet with a slice of crust. Heat olive oil in a large ovenproof sauté pan on high heat. Add sturgeon, then put the pan in the oven for 12 minutes until the crust is golden and the fish is cooked to medium doneness.

To serve In the centre of each of four plates, spread a large spoonful of the cauliflower purée. Top with a fillet of sturgeon, then arrange a quarter of the beets around the purée and drizzle each plate with a quarter of the sauce.

Suggested wine Try a more structured white Burgundy or lighter Oregon pinot noir.

Smoked Sturgeon

with Sauerkraut and Riesling Bacon Sauce

SERVES 4

- 1 Tbsp + 2 tsp olive oil
- 4 farm-raised sturgeon fillets, 5 oz each, skin removed
- 4 slices smoked fatty bacon
- 1 onion, thinly sliced
- 2 cups sauerkraut, rinsed and drained
- 1/2 bottle kabinett riesling (1 1/2 cups)
- 8 juniper berries, crushed
- 2 dried bay leaves
- 1/2 cup white wine sauce (page 188)
- 1/2 cup all-purpose flour
- Pinch of baking powder
- 1/2 cup sparkling water
- 1 egg yolk
- 1 cup + 3 Tbsp canola oil
- 2 egg whites
- 8 fresh bay leaves, rinsed and patted dry

The sturgeon in this recipe is cold-smoked, meaning that the smoking process does not cook the fish. You will need a cast-iron barbecue smoker and a handful of apple wood chips.

Put apple wood chips in a small cast-iron smoker and place the box on one side of the barbecue grill. Turn the heat on that side to maximum for 10 to 15 minutes with the lid closed until smoke appears.

Grease a flat pizza pan with 1 Tbsp of the olive oil and place sturgeon fillets on top. Fill a second pizza pan with a 1-inch layer of crushed ice. Top this pan with the first pan and transfer this entire assembly to the barbecue grill, at the opposite end to the smoker. Close the lid as quickly as possible to avoid losing too much smoke. Leave the heat on maximum for another minute, then turn off the heat. Keep the barbecue lid closed and allow the sturgeon fillets to smoke for 20 minutes until all of the smoke has disappeared.

In a large pot, render the bacon over low heat for about 2 minutes, then remove and set aside. Add onions and sweat for 5 minutes. Add sauerkraut, riesling, juniper berries and dried bay leaves. Cover this mixture with a cartouche—a circle of parchment paper cut to the diameter of the pot with a small hole cut in the centre to allow steam to escape—and simmer over medium-low heat for 1 hour.

Add white wine sauce, then bring back to a simmer. Strain the liquid into a medium saucepan. Keep the sauce and sauerkraut warm separately on low heat.

In a large mixing bowl, stir together flour, baking powder, sparkling water, egg yolk and 1 Tbsp of canola oil and allow this batter to rest, covered, for 30 minutes. Whip egg whites to soft peaks and fold them into the batter.

Heat 1 cup of the canola oil in a deep saucepan on medium-high heat. Pull each fresh bay leaf through the batter and, using tongs, place it in the hot oil. Fry bay leaves until batter is puffed and golden brown, about 30 seconds. Remove these beignets from the oil and allow them to drain on paper towels. Season with salt.

Preheat the oven to 400°F. Heat 2 Tbsp of canola oil in a large sauté pan on high heat. Season sturgeon fillets with salt and pepper and sear in the pan until golden, about 2 minutes. Turn the fillets and finish them in a convection oven for 6 to 8 minutes (or 10 to 15 minutes in a conventional oven).

Turn the broiler on. Place bacon on a baking sheet and broil until crisp.

To serve Season sauerkraut with salt and pepper and heap a quarter of it on each of four plates. Top with a sturgeon fillet.

Froth the sauce with a hand-held blender for one minute until foamy. Spoon a quarter of the sauce around each dish.

Garnish each dish with a slice of bacon and two bay leaf beignets. Don't eat the leaves—simply pull off the cooked batter with your teeth.

Suggested wine A bright sauvignon blanc from either Pouilly-Fumé or Dry Creek.

Spice-crusted Albacore Tuna Carpaccio

with Grilled Pineapple, Tomatillo and Coconut

SERVES 4

Spice-crusted tuna Grind Sichuan peppercorns, coriander seeds, black peppercorns and fennel seeds coarsely in a clean coffee grinder, then transfer them to a plate.

Season albacore loin with salt, then roll it in the spices, pressing down on the fish to get a thin coating of spices on all sides.

Heat olive oil in a large sauté pan on high heat. Add albacore and sear it for about 15 seconds on each side. The tuna should remain rare in the centre. Remove the tuna from the pan and place it on a paper towel to absorb any excess oil. Refrigerate immediately.

Once chilled, wrap the tuna very tightly in several layers of plastic wrap, which will make slicing the fish easier.

Salsa Preheat a grill to high, then grill pineapple slices until grill marks are visible on each side. Remove the pineapple to a dish and add rum. Refrigerate the dish for at least 10 minutes until chilled.

Cut out and discard the core from the pineapple and chop the pineapple into small dice, reserving all the juices. Add the remaining ingredients and season with salt and pepper. Refrigerate the salsa until ready to serve. Will keep refrigerated in an airtight container for up to 7 days.

Coconut cream Strain coconut milk through a gold tea filter, reserving the thick coconut cream. Whisk this cream with lime zest and refrigerate until ready to serve.

To serve With a long, thin-bladed knife, slice tuna as thinly as possible and place five slices in a circle on each of four plates. Discard the plastic wrap. Season the tuna with coarse sea salt and sprinkle with two tablespoons of the pineapple-tomatillo salsa and some of the marinade. Drizzle the coconut cream on top and finish with cilantro.

Suggested wine Try something lean with mineral and fruit, like a sauvignon blanc from Casablanca in Chile.

Spice-crusted tuna

- 1 Tbsp Sichuan peppercorns
- 1 Tbsp coriander seeds
- 1 Tbsp black peppercorns
- 1 Tbsp fennel seeds
- 14 oz albacore tuna loin
- 2 Tbsp olive oil
- 1/4 cup cilantro shoots or cilantro leaves, chiffonaded

Salsa

- 2 thin slices pineapple
- Dash of dark rum
- 3 tomatillos, finely diced
- 1/2 red bell pepper, seeded and finely diced
- 1/2 jalapeño pepper, seeded and finely diced
- 1 Tbsp crushed pink peppercorns
- 1 Tbsp finely diced red onion
- 1 tsp freshly grated ginger
- 1 green onion, thinly sliced
- Juice of 1 lime
- Dash of olive oil

Coconut cream

- 1 can (5 oz) coconut milk, unstirred
- Zest of 1 lime

Grilled Albacore Tuna

with Baby Bok Choy, Edamame and Shimeji Mushrooms

SERVES 4

Quinoa

¼ cup red quinoa seeds, well rinsed

Dumplings

8 spot prawns, peeled, deveined and chopped

4 Tbsp cooked red quinoa seeds

2 shiso leaves, stems removed and chopped

8 dumpling wrappers

Bok choy and mushrooms

2 Tbsp sesame oil

10 oz baby bok choy, washed and cut in half lengthwise

2 small carrots, peeled and thinly sliced

1 rib celery, thinly sliced

1 cluster shimeji mushrooms (about 4 oz)

2 oz shelled edamame beans

Grilled tuna

20 oz albacore tuna loin, cut in 4 pieces

2 Tbsp sesame oil

1 tsp shichimi togarashi (Japanese seven-spice seasoning)

Bonito broth

2 cups ginger-scented smoked bonito broth (page 186)

Dash of rice vinegar

Dash of yuzu juice

Dash of soy sauce

1 scallion, thinly sliced

1 tsp sesame seeds, toasted

Shimeji mushrooms have a slightly crunchy texture and a nutty taste and are best served cooked rather than raw. Quinoa is a grain grown largely in South America and looks like little spirals when it is cooked. The red variety has a slightly earthier flavour than the white one. Shichimi togarashi is a Japanese spice mixture made with seven ingredients, coarsely ground red chili pepper being the main component. If you cannot find it, cayenne will work just as well. This recipe also calls for shiso leaves, a popular Asian herb from the mint family. All these ingredients are available in specialty food stores.

Quinoa Combine quinoa seeds with a pinch of salt and ½ cup water. Bring to a boil on medium-high heat and cook for about 12 minutes until quinoa has absorbed all of the water.

Dumplings In a small bowl, combine prawns, quinoa and shiso. Season with salt and pepper.

Arrange the dumpling wrappers on a clean work surface. Place 1 Tbsp of the prawn mixture in the centre of each wrapper. Moisten the wrapper edges with a little water and fold them in half, pinching the edges to seal. Crimp the edges into a folding-fan shape and form the dumplings into half-moons.

Bring a medium pot of salted water to a boil. Add dumplings and cook for 30 seconds. Drain.

Bok choy and mushrooms Heat sesame oil in a large sauté pan on high heat. Add bok choy, carrots, celery, mushrooms and edamame beans, and sauté for 2 minutes until vegetables are lightly cooked but still crunchy. Remove from the heat, then season with salt and pepper.

Grilled tuna Brush tuna with sesame oil and season with togarashi and salt. Allow tuna to warm to room temperature.

Preheat a grill to medium-high. Grill tuna for 30 seconds on each side. The centre should be rare.

Bonito broth In a small pot, heat ginger-scented smoked bonito broth until warmed through. Season with the remaining ingredients.

To serve Heap a quarter of the stir-fried vegetables in the centre of each of four wide bowls. Using a very sharp knife, cut each piece of albacore into three pieces and place them on top of the vegetables. Pour a quarter of the savoury bonito broth on top and garnish with two dumplings.

Suggested wine Opt for an Eden Valley viognier that shows lean and bright fruit.

Smoked Albacore Tuna Terrine

with Green Apple and Sorrel Salad

SERVES 4

Riesling vinegar is a sweet wine vinegar; if it is not available, try a chardonnay vinegar. Smoked albacore is available from most fishmongers.

Terrine Whip together cream cheese and butter in a food processor until light and fluffy. Add ⅓ cup of the water, horseradish, lemon juice, salt, pepper and chives. Heat the remaining water in the microwave for 30 seconds. Press out excess moisture from the gelatin and dissolve it in the warm water. Stir this mixture into the cream cheese mix.

Line a 4-inch-deep terrine mould with plastic wrap, with the plastic extending from the edges by 4 inches on each side. Arrange a layer of smoked tuna in the terrine, with the slices going slightly up the sides. Cover with a thin layer of the cream cheese mixture. Continue to layer tuna and cream cheese, working quickly before the cream sets, until the terrine mould is full or you are running out of tuna. The top layer should be smoked tuna. Wrap the overhanging plastic wrap over the top layer and refrigerate for at least 6 hours.

Unmould the terrine on a cutting board and cut ¾-inch slices with the plastic wrap still on for easier handling. An electric knife works best, but you can also use a long, thin blade. Discard the plastic wrap after slicing.

Salad In a food processor, blend grapeseed oil, apple cider, vinegar, coarsely chopped apple and sugar until puréed and well mixed. Pass the purée through a fine-mesh sieve and season with salt and pepper.

To serve Mix diced apple, red onion, radishes and kohlrabi into the apple vinaigrette right before serving. Arrange a slice of smoked albacore terrine in the centre of each of four plates and surround it with two tablespoons of the salad and vinaigrette. Sprinkle each plate with a quarter of the fresh sorrel.

Suggested wine Try a sweeter white with fresh fruits and spices—gewürztraminer from the Okanagan Valley would work well.

Terrine

- 9 oz cream cheese, softened at room temperature
- 1/3 cup unsalted butter, softened at room temperature
- 1/2 cup water
- 2 Tbsp freshly grated horseradish
- Juice of 1/2 lemon
- 2 Tbsp minced chives
- 3 leaves gelatin, softened in a little cold water
- 18 oz cold-smoked albacore tuna, thinly sliced

Salad

- 1/2 cup grapeseed oil
- 3 Tbsp Okanagan hard apple cider
- 3 Tbsp riesling vinegar
- 1 Granny Smith apple, cored, then half coarsely chopped and the other half finely diced
- Pinch of sugar
- 1 Tbsp finely minced red onion
- 2 red radishes, julienned on a mandolin
- 2 very thin slices of kohlrabi, peeled and finely diced
- 4 large fresh sorrel leaves, stems removed, chiffonaded

Ling Cod with Chorizo Sauce

Served with Saffron Basmati Rice, Chickpeas and Squid

SERVES 4

Chickpeas

½ cup dried chickpeas
2 cups chicken stock (page 184)
1 Tbsp olive oil
½ small onion
1 small carrot
1 rib celery
1 clove garlic
1 sprig thyme

Cod and squid

2 tomatoes
4 ling cod fillets, 5 oz each, skin removed
4 Tbsp olive oil
6 small squid, tubes only, in very thin rings
1 clove garlic, minced
1 shallot, minced
¼ cup parsley, chiffonaded
½ cup cooked chickpeas, drained

Chickpeas Soak dried chickpeas in a bowl of water at room temperature for 24 hours, then drain. In a pressure cooker, combine chickpeas, chicken stock, olive oil, onion, carrot, celery, garlic and thyme and cook for 10 to 15 minutes (or cook them over medium heat on the stove for 45 minutes to 1 hour). Season the chickpeas in their cooking liquid with salt and pepper and refrigerate them overnight.

Cod and squid Fill a bowl with ice water. Bring a medium pot of water to a boil. Add tomatoes and blanch for 10 seconds. Remove them from the water and plunge them into the ice bath. Peel the tomatoes, then cut them in half and remove the seeds. Dice the tomato flesh and set it aside in a bowl.

Season ling cod fillets with salt and pepper. Heat 2 Tbsp of the olive oil in a sauté pan on medium-high heat, then add the ling cod fillets. Sear for 3 to 4 minutes on each side until both sides have a golden crust and the fish is cooked to medium or medium rare.

Pat squid rings dry with a kitchen towel. Heat 1 Tbsp of the olive oil in a sauté pan on high heat. Add garlic, shallot and squid rings. Toss quickly and cook for 15 seconds, then add parsley and transfer this squid mixture to a bowl. Heat the pan again with the remaining 1 Tbsp of olive oil. Add tomatoes and cook for about 15 seconds over high heat. Add chickpeas and cook for 1 minute. Add this mixture to the squid rings and toss to combine.

Chorizo sauce Preheat the oven to 350°F. In a baking dish, toss tomatoes and red bell pepper with 2 Tbsp of the olive oil, salt and pepper. Roast for 30 minutes. Turn the tomatoes and bell pepper and cook for another 30 minutes.

Heat 1 Tbsp of the olive oil in a saucepan on high heat. Add chorizo and cook for 3 minutes. Add onion and garlic to the rendered fat and cook for 2 minutes. Add roasted tomatoes and bell pepper, wine and bouquet garni, then season with salt and pepper and cook for 20 minutes. Remove the bouquet garni, transfer the sauce to a blender and purée. Pass the sauce through a fine-mesh sieve, then season with salt and pepper.

Chorizo sauce

- 10 Roma tomatoes, halved and seeded
- 1 red bell pepper, chopped and seeded
- 3 Tbsp olive oil
- 1 chorizo sausage, diced
- 1 small onion, minced
- 2 cloves garlic, chopped
- 1 cup white wine
- 2 sprigs fresh oregano, 2 sprigs thyme, 1 sprig basil and 1 bay leaf, tied into a bouquet garni

Basmati rice

- ½ cup basmati rice
- ¾ cup water
- 1 Tbsp unsalted butter
- 1 pod star anise
- 1 tsp saffron

Basmati rice Rinse basmati rice several times in a bowl, using fresh water each time, until the water runs clear. Drain the rice. In a medium pot, combine the rice and the water and bring them to a boil on high heat. Add butter, star anise, saffron and a pinch of salt. Reduce the heat to low, cover the pot and cook for 10 minutes. Turn off the heat and the allow the rice to finish cooking for another 5 minutes. Remove the star anise and fluff the rice with a fork.

To serve Spoon a quarter of the chorizo sauce on each of four plates, slightly off centre. Arrange a quarter of the squid and chickpeas on top of the sauce, then top with a fillet of ling cod. On the side, place a quarter of the saffron basmati rice.

Suggested wine Focus on spice with sweet fruit; try a pinot noir from the Okanagan Valley or a lighter Rhône wine.

Ling Cod

with Confit of Artichokes, Fennel, Cipollini Onions and Green Olives

SERVES 4

- 1 lemon, halved
- 4 artichokes
- 1 bulb fennel
- 2 nugget potatoes
- 4 fillets ling cod, 5 oz each, skin and bones removed
- 4 Tbsp kosher salt
- ½ cup + 2 tsp extra-virgin olive oil
- 3 anchovy fillets, rinsed and chopped
- 8 cloves garlic
- 1 cup dark chicken stock (page 185)
- 8 cipollini onions, peeled and quartered
- 1 cup chicken stock (page 184)
- 1 sprig thyme
- 1 bay leaf
- 12 green olives, pitted and halved
- 12 grape tomatoes, halved
- 2 sprigs Italian parsley, leaves picked off and stems discarded
- Sprigs of fresh herbs, such as parsley or dill, for garnish

Prepare a bowl of acidulated water by squeezing the juice of half a lemon into a large bowl of cold water.

Break off the outer leaves of each artichoke and trim the remaining leaves with a knife until you reach the heart. Discard the artichoke leaves. Halve each artichoke heart, then scrape out the choke with a spoon. Cut each artichoke half into four wedges. Reserve in the acidulated water.

Cut off the root end of the fennel bulb and peel off the large outer layers, leaving the heart intact. Discard the root end and the outer layers. Cut off and discard the tough parts of the stem, then cut the fennel pieces and the heart into ¼-inch slices.

Quarter nugget potatoes and set them aside in cold water.

Place fish on a baking sheet, cover with a layer of kosher salt and allow them to cure for 10 minutes. Rinse thoroughly and dry on a kitchen towel.

In a small saucepan, warm 4 Tbsp of olive oil on low heat with the anchovies and 6 garlic cloves. Cook for 20 minutes until the anchovies fall apart and the garlic is soft. Add dark chicken stock, then cook until the liquid has reduced by half, about 10 minutes. Pass this sauce through a fine-mesh sieve into a bowl, then season with a squeeze of lemon juice.

Pat the potato and artichoke wedges dry with a kitchen towel. Heat 2 Tbsp of olive oil on high heat in a wide pot. Add potato wedges and cook for 5 minutes until cut sides are golden brown. Add artichoke hearts, cook for 5 minutes, and season with salt and pepper. Add fennel slices, cipollini onions and the remaining 2 garlic cloves and cook for 2 minutes. Add chicken stock, thyme and bay leaf and cover the pot with a lid. Cook for 12 minutes on medium-low heat until all vegetables are tender.

Once the vegetables are tender, add olives, tomatoes, parsley and 2 tsp of extra-virgin olive oil. Remove thyme and bay leaf and keep the pot warm on low heat.

In a large sauté pan, heat 2 Tbsp olive oil on high. Add ling cod and cook for 6 minutes until golden brown on both sides, partly covering the pan to prevent oil from splattering.

To serve Arrange a quarter of the vegetable confit just off centre on each of four plates. Place the ling cod fillet beside it, drizzle anchovy sauce around the dish, and garnish with herbs.

Suggested wine Try a chardonnay from Côte Chalonnaise.

Baked Ling Cod

with Tomato-Caper Fondue and Smoked Eggplant Purée

SERVES 4

- 8 large Roma tomatoes
- 1/2 cup + 2 Tbsp or more extra-virgin olive oil
- 3 cloves garlic, finely chopped
- 2 shallots, finely diced
- Zest of 1 lemon
- 5 leaves basil, 3 of them chiffonaded
- 1 Tbsp capers, rinsed and chopped
- 8 leaves Italian parsley, chiffonaded
- Pinch of espelette pepper
- 1 large Italian eggplant
- 1/4 onion, chopped
- 1/2 jalapeño pepper, seeded and chopped
- 1 sprig thyme
- Dash of red wine vinegar
- 1/2 lemon
- 4 Tbsp panko (Japanese bread crumbs)
- 4 ling cod fillets, 5 oz each, skin and pinbones removed
- Pinch of fennel pollen (or coarsely ground fennel seeds)

Fennel pollen imparts a very sweet fennel taste. It is available in specialty food stores, but if you cannot find fennel pollen, substitute coarsely ground fennel seeds. Use any eggplant purée leftover from this recipe as a dip with crackers.

Fill a bowl with ice water. Bring a large pot of water to a boil. Add tomatoes and blanch for 10 seconds, then plunge them into the ice bath. Peel and seed the tomatoes and cut the flesh into ¼-inch dice.

In a medium sauté pan, heat 4 Tbsp of the olive oil on medium heat. Add ⅓ of the garlic and sauté until it becomes fragrant and just begins to brown, about 30 seconds, then add shallots. Cook for 30 more seconds and add tomatoes, lemon zest and the 2 whole basil leaves. Cook over low heat for about 30 minutes, stirring regularly, until all of the tomato water has evaporated and the fondue starts to thicken. Add capers and parsley and season with salt and espelette pepper, then refrigerate this fondue.

Preheat a grill to medium-high. Grill eggplant whole, with the lid down, until all 4 sides are well charred and a smoky flavour develops, about 7 minutes per side. The eggplant should be very soft to the touch. Remove from the heat and set aside.

In a medium pot, heat 2 Tbsp of the olive oil on medium heat. Add onion, jalapeño, thyme and the remaining garlic and cook for 5 to 10 minutes until fragrant and lightly browned.

Cut the cooked eggplant in half, scoop out the flesh and add it to the onion mixture. Discard the eggplant skins. Continue to cook the eggplant mixture until all liquid has evaporated, about 10 minutes, then remove the thyme and add vinegar.

Blend this mixture in a food processor with 3 Tbsp of your best extra-virgin olive oil, then strain the purée through a sieve—use a plastic-mesh sieve to avoid oxidation. Add chiffonaded basil and season with salt and pepper and a squeeze of lemon juice. Set aside.

In a small bowl, toss together panko and 1 Tbsp of olive oil.

Preheat the oven to 425°F. Season ling cod fillets with salt, pepper and fennel pollen (or fennel seeds) and place them on a baking sheet. Cover each fillet with a layer of the tomato fondue, top with a thin layer of panko and bake the ling cod for 12 to 15 minutes until the fish is just done and the crust is golden.

To serve Spread one large spoonful of eggplant purée in the centre of each of four plates. Top with a ling cod fillet and finish the dish with a drizzle of extra-virgin olive oil.

Suggested wine A lighter red with dried-fruit aromas, such as a Chianti Classico.

SHELLFISH

SHELLFISH

IN EACH SHELL is a pearl of sorts—especially at Blue Water Cafe, where fresh, often live shellfish yield their hidden treasure to diners. Shellfish large and small are bountiful in the Pacific region, and, owing in large part to sustainable harvest practices, their future looks healthy.

Crabs have twelve edible species in the waters of the Pacific Northwest, but king and Dungeness are the most important commercially. The season begins early in the year, rises in intensity by late spring and finishes by early August. At Blue Water Cafe, king crabs are welcomed for their large legs and corresponding amount of meat. Dungeness crabs, as judged by their nearly iconic status in restaurants from fine to humble, are the popular choice for their pure, delicate flavour and myriad preparations, from simply boiled and served with drawn butter to accompanied by the most elaborate sauces and garnishes. A large tank to the side of the kitchen at the Blue Water Cafe contains live specimens, often astonishingly large. This is not merely for show; these creatures will arrive at the table in the best possible condition, and the preparation of the day will show the delicate meat to great effect.

Spot prawns, part of the Pandalid family, are the culinary rock stars of the Pacific Northwest during early summer, a season that lasts roughly one month from early May each year. They are found on rocky ocean bottoms, covering a range from nearly intertidal to depths of over 295 feet, where they apply their foraging skills. Caught in species-specific traps, spot prawns are a sustainable delicacy and well worth the celebration when their season begins. The meat is tender but with some good resistance in the mouth, sweet yet retaining an essence of the sea, in some ways like a more tender lobster meat. Blue Water Cafe, along with its sister restaurant West, celebrates spot prawn season each year and was one of the founders of the annual Spot Prawn Festival held in Vancouver.

Lobsters, solitary and nocturnal, are the world's largest marine crustaceans, reaching weights of 44 pounds at the august age of fifty-plus years, although the optimum size for eating is closer to 1½ pounds, when the meat is both abundant and flavourful, with a firm texture. American lobsters—also known as Atlantic, Maine or northern lobsters—are best consumed fresh, taken live from the water. Thanks to shipping prowess being what it is, live lobsters arrive daily on the West Coast. Nova Scotia is Blue Water Cafe's main source. Although prime eating season is considered to be late autumn after the tourist season has dissipated, lobsters are available year-round. Chefs prize these shellfish for their delicate flavours and abundant meat in both the claws and the tail. Seasoned lobster aficionados will tell you that various parts of the carapace hold many tasty morsels as well.

Clams are bivalve molluscs, and the catch-all term "clam" refers, basically, to any bivalve that is not an oyster, mussel or scallop. Restaurants use three main types of clams—littlenecks, the established but non-indigenous Manila and the recently introduced non-indigenous savoury (also known as varnish or purple mahogany)—all of which have a common trait: they must be alive at the time of shucking and/or cooking. Littlenecks are considered to yield a somewhat more delicate and flavourful meat, while Manilas offer a greater meat-to-shell ratio and grow faster. The vividly purple savouries—introduced to the Pacific

Northwest in the early 1990s via some ballast bilge water from a cargo vessel—have captured the visual imagination of chefs and diners alike and by consensus provide a somewhat creamier, richer texture than the others. Plus, this shellfish is adaptable to a wide variety of preparations and is ideally suited to cultivation and farming.

Mussels, like clams, must be alive when shucked and/or cooked. Mussels boast a larger meat-to-shell ratio (often near 60 per cent) and have a creamier, more unctuous texture than clams. So, preparation is everything—to retain and showcase the briny, fresh bivalve flavour without overdoing it. Quadra Island is home to a hybrid species called Honey Mussel, a unique cultivation derived from a special selection of exotic and local mussels. The result: a pristine, succulent, sweet-as-honey product that is ideal for cooking—an instant hit with chefs. Ebony mussels, also farmed just off Quadra, are brinier and perhaps more versatile. In this region, they are pristine and adaptable.

Oysters in British Columbia were, until recently, considered inferior to those available in Seattle or on the East Coast. But the tide has turned in a big way. Local oysters have become some of the world's finest. Late fall to early spring, in particular, is prime harvesting time, and because oysters are so responsive to their particular growing place, subtle differences exist throughout the region. Individual oyster cultivators promote their particular and unique qualities, and consumers are the better for all of it. Most are Pacific oysters, which are offspring of oysters originally living around Japan (the Olympia variety is the only species of oyster native to the Northwest), but cultivators have also had great success with the Japanese kusshi oyster, which packs a great deal of delicate flavour in its smaller package.

Scallops have the distinction of being the one bivalve that generally stands the "I hate bivalves" test. Their dense, rich meat, or more accurately their central adductor muscle, is what we associate with the scallop, although the muscle is a relatively small part of the entire creature. Scallops are free-swimming, so they actually grow and use this muscle as part of a water intake and expulsion process—a kind of miniature jet-propulsion system; hence the muscle's size. Pacific scallops can grow very large and are available to chefs in four ascending weights, from small to great. With the advent of successful sustainable cultivation methods, scallops are available all year long.

Dungeness Crab Bisque

SERVES 4

- 2 whole Dungeness crabs, each about $2\frac{1}{2}$ lbs
- 1/3 cup olive oil
- 1 onion, sliced
- 1 rib celery, sliced
- 1 small carrot, sliced
- 1 bulb of garlic, unpeeled but halved
- 3 Tbsp unsalted butter
- 1/3 cup brandy
- 1/3 cup dry sherry
- 4 Tbsp tomato paste
- 1 tomato, diced
- 3 sprigs thyme, 2 sprigs tarragon, 2 sprigs parsley and 1 bay leaf, tied into a bouquet garni
- 8 cups fish stock (page 186)
- 5 Tbsp basmati or jasmine rice
- 2 cups water
- 1 cup whipping cream
- Pinch of cayenne pepper
- 1/3 cup whipped cream
- Tarragon leaves to taste, for garnish
- Sprigs of chervil, for garnish

Fill a large bowl with ice water. Bring a large pot of salted water to a boil on high heat. Add crabs and cook for 2 minutes. Remove 1 crab from the water and plunge it into the ice bath. Cook the second crab for 13 minutes more, then plunge it into the ice bath.

Grasping both the body and the legs of the 2-minute-cooked crab with one hand, pull off the shell with the other hand. Spoon out and reserve the crab viscera (all of the contents of the shell), then discard the shell.

With a heavy chef's knife, cut the crab body into 2-inch pieces, cutting through all the leg pieces and shoulder parts. Remove the crab meat from the shells, then place all the pieces in a colander over a bowl, and collect any liquid that drains from the crab.

In a large pot, heat olive oil on high heat. Add onion, celery, carrot and garlic and sauté until lightly browned, 5 to 10 minutes. Remove the vegetables from the pot and set them aside. Add butter to the pot, followed by the crab pieces, and cook until crab starts to brown, 10 to 15 minutes.

Deglaze the pot with brandy and sherry, cook for 2 minutes to allow alcohol to evaporate, then add tomato paste and diced tomato. Cook for 5 minutes, then add the reserved vegetables and the bouquet garni.

Using a knife or a nutcracker, crack the shells of the 15-minute-cooked crab, pick out the meat and reserve it for the garnish. Add the shells to the pot.

Add fish stock, crab viscera and any strained liquids from the crab. Reduce the heat to low, add rice and simmer for 45 minutes, or until liquid has reduced by half. Strain the liquid into another pot. Return the solids to the first pot and add the 2 cups of water. Cook for another 10 minutes and strain again into the pot with the liquid.

Press on the solids to extract all the crab juices. Discard the solids. Add whipping cream to the liquid, then bring this soup back to a boil on medium-high heat and season with salt and cayenne.

To serve Place a quarter cup of the bisque in a small saucepan, add the reserved crab meat and heat gently on medium heat. Arrange this mixture in the centre of four bowls. Whisk whipped cream into the bisque and sprinkle with fresh tarragon leaves. Ladle around the crab meat and garnish with a sprig of chervil.

Suggested wine A sherry would be strong enough to match this bisque—stay with a fino style.

Gazpacho and Zucchini Blossoms

Stuffed with Dungeness Crab

SERVES 4

Gazpacho

- 2 Tbsp sherry vinegar
- 1/4 cup extra-virgin olive oil
- 1 slice stale foccacia
- 1 large red bell pepper, seeded and roughly chopped
- 1 large ripe tomato, roughly chopped
- 1/4 English cucumber, roughly chopped
- 1 green onion, roughly chopped
- 1/4 jalapeño pepper, seeded and roughly chopped
- 1 small clove garlic, germ removed, roughly chopped
- 1 sprig each basil, Italian parsley and fresh thyme, tied into a bouquet garni

Gazpacho In a small bowl, combine vinegar and olive oil. Place foccacia in the vinaigrette and allow to soak for 15 minutes. (It is not necessary for all the vinegar and oil to have been absorbed.)

Place red bell pepper, tomato, cucumber, green onion, jalapeño, garlic and the soaked foccacia in a blender and purée. Strain the mixture through a fine-mesh sieve, season with salt and pepper, add bouquet garni and refrigerate for at least 2 hours. Will keep refrigerated in an airtight container for up to 5 days.

Stuffed zucchini blossoms Purée sea scallops in a food processor, add whipping cream and blend just long enough to emulsify the mixture. Pass this purée though a fine-mesh sieve and fold in whipped cream. Season with salt, freshly ground pepper and a squeeze of lemon juice.

In a small sauté pan, heat olive oil on high heat. Add shallot, garlic, zucchini, red bell pepper and half a yellow bell pepper and sauté for about 5 minutes until vegetables are cooked but still slightly crunchy. Add Pernod and tarragon. Cook for another 30 seconds, then refrigerate until chilled, about 30 minutes.

Fold crab meat and chilled vegetable mix into the scallop mousse and transfer this mixture to a piping bag. Stuff all the zucchini blossoms with the crab mixture. Do not fill them more than two-thirds full. Fold the zucchini flower tips over the opening to form small packages.

Steam stuffed zucchini flowers in a bamboo steamer over boiling water for 10 minutes until stuffing is cooked. Remove from the heat and refrigerate until ready to serve.

Zucchini blossom tempura In a bowl, mix together flour, sparkling water and baking powder, being careful not to overmix—the tempura batter can be a little lumpy.

Heat vegetable oil in a deep pot or a deep fryer to 350°F. Pull each zucchini blossom through the chickpea flour, dusting off the excess. Then pull the blossom through the tempura batter and allow the excess to drip off. Fry zucchini blossoms in the hot oil until crispy, about 10 seconds per side. Carefully remove the blossoms using tongs, drain on several layers of paper towel and season with salt.

To serve Divide gazpacho among four well-chilled soup bowls. At the centre of each bowl, arrange three stuffed zucchini blossoms in a star shape. Between the flowers, arrange the reserved crab pieces. Drizzle extra-virgin olive oil overtop and garnish each bowl with a tempura zucchini blossom and a sprinkling of the remaining diced yellow pepper.

Suggested wine A gewürztraminer from Alsace.

Stuffed zucchini blossoms

- 3 oz Pacific sea scallops
- 4 Tbsp whipping cream
- 1/4 cup whipped cream
- 1/2 lemon
- 1 Tbsp olive oil + extra for garnish
- 1 shallot, minced
- 1 clove garlic, germ removed, chopped
- 4 oz zucchini, finely diced
- 1/2 red bell pepper, seeded and finely diced
- 3/4 yellow bell pepper, seeded and finely diced
- Dash of Pernod
- 2 tsp minced tarragon leaves
- 9 oz Dungeness crab meat, picked over to remove small shell pieces and 12 larger pieces set aside for garnish
- 12 large male zucchini blossoms, stamens and stems removed

Zucchini blossom tempura

- 1/4 cup chickpea flour + extra for dredging
- 1/2 cup ice-cold sparkling water
- Pinch of baking powder
- 4 cups vegetable oil, for deep-frying
- 4 large male zucchini flowers, stamens and stems removed, cut open on one side and fanned out

facing: Dungeness Crab and Corn Salad
with Sunflower Sprouts

Dungeness Crab and Corn Salad

with Sunflower Sprouts

SERVES 4

Red pepper jelly

- 2 red bell peppers
- 1 Roma tomato
- 2 Tbsp olive oil
- 1 shallot, minced
- 1 clove garlic, minced
- 1 sprig basil
- 1 sprig thyme
- Zest of 1/4 orange
- Dash of hot chili purée
- 1 Tbsp sherry vinegar
- 1/4 cup water
- Pinch of sugar
- 1/16 oz agar-agar

Sunflower sprouts, fennel pollen and borage flowers are available at farmer's markets and specialty food stores, where you will also find hot chili purée.

Red pepper jelly Preheat a grill to high. Place red bell peppers directly on the grill and cook, turning occasionally, until the skins are lightly charred on all sides. Remove from the heat, place in a covered bowl and let cool. Using a sharp knife, remove and discard the peel and seeds.

Fill a bowl with ice water. Bring a small pot of water to a boil on high heat. Add tomato and blanch for 30 seconds, then plunge it into the ice bath. Peel the tomato, then cut it in half and discard the seeds.

In a small sauté pan, heat olive oil on medium heat. Add shallot and garlic and cook until fragrant, about 1 minute. Add red bell pepper, tomato, basil, thyme, orange zest, chili purée, vinegar, water, sugar and a pinch of salt and simmer for 15 minutes. Remove the basil and thyme, then transfer the red pepper mixture to a blender and purée. Pass the purée through a fine-mesh sieve and season with salt and pepper. Measure 1 cup of the red pepper liquid into a small pot, add agar-agar and bring it back to a simmer. Cook for 2 minutes, stirring constantly. Pour this mixture into a container and refrigerate for 1 hour or until set.

Unmould the jelly and cut in ½-inch dice.

Crab and corn salad In a large bowl, gently toss together crab meat, corn kernels, green onions, celery, red bell pepper, jalapeño, cucumber, chervil, fennel pollen and a pinch of salt with your fingertips.

Orange-basil vinaigrette Combine all ingredients and a pinch of salt in a blender and emulsify. Strain this vinaigrette through a fine-mesh sieve into a bowl. Will keep refrigerated in an airtight container for up to 7 days.

Crab and corn salad

- 7 oz Dungeness crab meat, picked over to remove small shell pieces
- Kernels from 1 large cob of corn, cooked (about 4 oz)
- 4 green onions, thinly sliced
- 2 ribs celery, peeled and finely diced
- 1 small red bell pepper, seeded and finely diced
- ½ green jalapeño pepper, seeded and minced
- ¼ English cucumber, seeds removed and finely diced
- 1 Tbsp minced chervil
- Pinch of fennel pollen
- ¼ cup red pepper jelly
- 2 oz sunflower sprouts
- 20 borage flowers
- Pinch of espelette pepper

Orange-basil vinaigrette

- ⅓ cup olive oil
- 1 Tbsp concentrated orange juice
- Juice of 1 lime
- 1 ripe tomato
- 5 basil leaves
- Pinch of espelette pepper

To serve Season the crab and corn salad with six tablespoons of the vinaigrette. Toss gently with your fingertips, keeping the salad light and airy. In the centre of each of four plates, place a quarter of the salad in a 3-inch ring mould. Remove the ring mould. Drizzle extra vinaigrette around the dish. Place a quarter of the red pepper jelly cubes on the vinaigrette. Sprinkle each dish with a quarter of the sunflower sprouts and borage flowers and finish with a sprinkle of espelette pepper.

Suggested wine Try an unoaked chardonnay from B.C. or a Chablis.

Alaskan King Crab Panna Cotta

with Caviar Beurre Blanc

SERVES 4

- 1/2 tsp canola oil
- 1/2 cup white wine
- 1/4 cup Noilly Prat
- 1 Tbsp champagne vinegar
- 3 shallots, minced
- Zest of 1 lemon
- 1 cup whipping cream
- Pinch of cayenne pepper
- 1/16 oz agar-agar
- 7 oz cooked king crab meat, diced
- 1 Tbsp chopped chervil
- 4 Tbsp beurre blanc (page 188), warmed
- 1 oz Canadian sturgeon caviar
- 1/2 lemon
- 1 Tbsp minced chives
- 4 pieces cooked king crab meat, each 3 inches, for garnish
- Chervil sprigs to taste, for garnish

Lightly brush four 3-inch ramekins with canola oil.

In a small saucepan, combine wine, Noilly Prat, vinegar, shallots and lemon zest and heat on medium heat until liquid has reduced by three-quarters, about 10 minutes. Add cream and cayenne, bring to a simmer and strain through a fine-mesh sieve into a clean saucepan. Season to taste with salt and pepper, add agar-agar and cook for 2 minutes, stirring constantly. Pour the mixture over the crab meat, add chopped chervil and stir carefully. Spoon the panna cotta mixture into the ramekins and refrigerate.

In a small bowl, combine beurre blanc with caviar. Add a squeeze of lemon juice and chives.

To serve Before serving, preheat the oven to 300°F. Place the ramekins of panna cotta in a large roasting pan. Fill the roasting pan with water so that it reaches halfway up the sides of the ramekins, then place this pan in the oven for five minutes or until the panna cottas are warmed through. Remove from the oven.

To unmould the panna cottas, place a warm plate over each ramekin and carefully invert the plate and the ramekin together. Spoon a quarter of the caviar beurre blanc around each serving. Garnish with a piece of king crab meat and chervil sprigs.

Suggested wine Try a weightier white wine, such as a richer chardonnay from the Russian River Valley.

Alaskan King Crab

in Coconut Green Curry Sauce

SERVES 4 TO 6

Curry paste

- 4 to 6 green chilies, seeded and roughly chopped
- 2 shallots, roughly chopped
- 2-inch piece of fresh ginger, peeled and grated
- 2 cloves garlic, crushed
- 1 small bunch fresh cilantro, stalks and roots attached (if possible)
- 2 stalks lemon grass, chopped
- Zest and juice of 1 lime
- 8 kaffir lime leaves, torn into pieces
- 1-inch piece of galangal, peeled and chopped
- 1 Tbsp coriander seeds, crushed
- 1 tsp ground cumin
- 2 tsp Thai fish sauce
- 3 Tbsp olive oil

Curry sauce

- 1 king crab, 5 lbs
- 1 Tbsp vegetable oil
- 2 Tbsp green curry paste
- 1 Tbsp soft dark brown sugar
- 6 to 8 kaffir lime leaves, torn into pieces
- 1 can (13½ oz) coconut milk
- Dash of Thai fish sauce
- ¼ cup fresh cilantro, roughly chopped
- Juice of ½ lime

Jasmine rice

- 1¼ cups jasmine rice
- 1½ cups water
- 1 Tbsp butter

Curry paste Place all of the ingredients in a food processor and purée until the mixture becomes a paste. Will keep refrigerated in an airtight container for up to 2 weeks.

Curry sauce Fill a large bowl with ice water. Bring a large pot of salted water to a boil on high heat. Add crab and cook for 10 minutes, remove from the water and refresh in the ice bath.

Working over a sink and using a sharp knife, remove the head shell and wash off all innards under running water. Cut off the pair of claws and the 3 pairs of legs from the shoulder parts. Cut legs and claws in two pieces. With a small paring knife, make incisions through the length of the legs and claws to make it easier later to extract the crab meat. Cut the shoulder part into 8 pieces. Set aside.

Heat the vegetable oil in a wok or a large sauté pan on high heat. Add green curry paste and sugar and cook for about 1 minute, stirring constantly with a wooden spoon. Reduce the heat to medium and stir in the lime leaves and the shoulder meat from the crab until they are coated in the paste. Add coconut milk and fish sauce and bring to a simmer, cooking for 8 minutes. Add crab legs and claws and cook for another 5 minutes, until the sauce is thickened slightly. Stir in cilantro and lime juice, then season with more fish sauce if needed. (If the sauce is too spicy, add some more sugar; if it is not spicy enough, fry a little more curry paste in some oil for a minute or two and add to the sauce.)

Remove the curry from the heat and allow it to sit for a few minutes so the sauce becomes creamier. The true flavours of the curry paste ingredients will shine through as the sauce cools slightly.

Jasmine rice Rinse jasmine rice several times in a bowl, using fresh water each time, until the water runs clear. Drain the rice. In a medium pot, combine the rice and the water and bring them to a boil on high heat. Add butter and a pinch of salt. Reduce the heat to low, cover the pot and cook for 10 minutes. Turn off the heat and allow the rice to finish cooking for another 5 minutes. Fluff the rice with a fork.

To serve Arrange a quarter of the rice on each of four plates. Top each serving with a quarter of the crab and coconut green curry sauce.

Suggested wine A gewürztraminer from Alsace or from the Marlborough.

Spot Prawns

in a Cardamom and Kumquat Broth

SERVES 4

- 2 lbs fresh spot prawns
- 4 Tbsp olive oil
- 12 kumquats
- 3 shallots, sliced
- 2 cloves garlic, sliced
- 3/4 bulb fennel, 1/4 sliced and 1/2 diced
- 1-inch piece of ginger, peeled and sliced
- 2 Tbsp tomato paste
- 1 fresh tomato, chopped
- 1 cup Noilly Prat
- 2 sprigs thyme
- 4 cups fish stock (page 186)
- 1 Tbsp cardamom seeds, toasted and crushed
- 1/2 Tbsp fennel seeds, toasted
- Pinch of espelette pepper
- 2 green onions, thinly sliced

Separate the spot prawn tails from the heads and keep the tails chilled.

Set your stove exhaust to the highest setting. In a medium pot, heat olive oil on high heat until it starts to smoke slightly. Wearing an oven mitt or using a set of tongs, carefully add spot prawn heads (be careful not to burn yourself with the spattering oil). Crush the heads with a potato masher and cook until they start to brown, about 5 minutes, stirring occasionally.

Meanwhile, peel the kumquats and finely julienne the zest. Reserve the flesh.

Reduce the heat to medium and add shallots, garlic, sliced fennel and ginger. Cook until the vegetables are soft and fragrant, about 2 minutes. Add tomato paste and chopped tomato and cook for 5 minutes. Add Noilly Prat and cook until liquid has reduced by half, 4 to 5 minutes, then add thyme and fish stock. Add cardamom, fennel seeds, espelette pepper and the kumquat flesh. Cover and simmer gently on low heat for 20 minutes.

Strain the broth through a fine-mesh sieve into another pot, pressing gently to extract all of the essence from the prawn heads. Discard the solids. Skim off any oil from the surface. Bring the broth back to a simmer and allow to infuse, covered, for 30 minutes. Season with salt.

Increase the heat to medium-high and bring the broth to a boil. Add diced fennel and cook for 1 minute. Reduce the heat to low. Peel and devein the spot prawn tails, then cook in the broth for 30 seconds.

To serve Ladle a quarter of the broth and prawn tails into each of four bowls. Garnish with green onion and kumquat zest.

Suggested wine One with good acidity and mature fruit notes, like Fiano di Avellino from Campania.

Spot Prawns

with Samphire and Miso-Yuzu Sauce

SERVES 4

- 16 fresh jumbo spot prawns
- 7 oz samphire
- 1/4 cup sake
- 3 Tbsp shiro miso (white miso paste)
- 1/4 cup beurre blanc (page 188)
- 1 Tbsp yuzu juice
- 2 cups canola oil, for deep-frying
- 1/2 cup cornstarch
- 2 Tbsp olive oil
- Pinch of shichimi togarashi (Japanese seven-spice seasoning) or cayenne pepper

This recipe calls for shiro miso, a light-coloured miso paste made with rice, available at Asian supermarkets. It also calls for samphire, also known as sea asparagus or Salicornia, which you can buy at specialty food stores. Look for vibrant green stalks without brown spots or limpness. If you cannot find sea asparagus, substitute pencil-thin spears of green asparagus.

Remove the prawn tails from the heads and peel off the shell, leaving the tail segment attached to the meat. Set aside the heads. Arrange the prawn tails in a single layer, backs up, on a small baking sheet lined with parchment paper. With a sharp paring knife, make an incision lengthwise along the back of each prawn, then open it and use the tip of your knife to remove and discard any entrails.

Remove and discard the shell from the prawn heads, reserving the innards of the heads in a small bowl. Thoroughly wash the prawn bodies in cold water to remove any sand. Set aside to dry on a kitchen towel.

Fill a large bowl with ice water. Bring a large pot of water to a boil on high heat. Wash samphire and, with a sharp knife, remove and discard the tough end of each sprig. Place samphire in the boiling water and cook for 15 seconds. Refresh immediately in the ice bath to keep its vibrant green colour.

To make the sauce, heat sake in a small pot on medium heat. Add the innards of the prawn heads and cook for 1 minute. Remove from the heat and stir in shiro miso, then transfer to a small food processor and purée. Strain this mixture through a fine-mesh sieve into a pot, then add beurre blanc and yuzu juice. Season to taste.

Heat canola oil in a deep sauté pan on high heat until it reaches 350°F (use a thermometer to test the temperature). In a small bowl, toss prawn bodies in cornstarch, shaking off any excess. Fry prawns for 30 seconds until they crisp and start to become golden. Using tongs, remove from the oil and drain on paper towels. Season with salt.

To serve Gently heat the sauce on medium-low heat. Add samphire and heat until warmed through, then divide the sauce among four warmed appetizer plates.

Preheat the oven to 400°F. Place prawn tails on a baking sheet, season with salt and drizzle with olive oil. Bake for two to three minutes, until just about cooked. Arrange four prawn tails on top of each serving of samphire. Spoon sauce over the tails and arrange crispy prawn bodies randomly on the plate. Garnish with a sprinkle of shichimi togarashi (or cayenne).

Suggested wine A lighter white wine with dried-fruit aroma, such as a British Columbia pinot auxerrois.

Lobsters Poached in Tarragon Nage

with Seasonal Vegetables

SERVES 4

- 1 cup vegetable stock
- 1 cup beurre blanc (page 188)
- 2 sprigs tarragon, leaves only
- 4 baby carrots, peeled and cut in 1/4-inch slices
- 4 small fingerling potatoes, cut in 1/4-inch slices
- 1/4 lb yellow wax beans, cut in 1-inch pieces
- 1/4 lb haricots verts (tiny green beans), cut in 1/4-inch pieces
- 4 stalks broccolini, flowers only, cut in 1-inch pieces
- 1/4 lb green peas, shucked
- 1/4 lb fava beans, shucked
- 4 Nova Scotia lobsters, 1 1/2 lbs each
- 1/2 lemon

Bring vegetable stock to a boil on medium-high heat. Whisk the beurre blanc into vegetable stock and season with salt and pepper. Reduce the heat to low, stir in tarragon leaves and keep the nage warm while you prepare the vegetables.

Fill a large bowl with ice water. Bring 24 cups of salted water to a boil in a large pot. Add carrots and cook until slightly crunchy, about 3 minutes. Remove carrots from the water and plunge them into the ice bath. Repeat with the potatoes (about 10 minutes), wax beans and haricots verts (each about 2 minutes), and broccolini, green peas and fava beans (each about 1 minute), cooking each vegetable individually in the salted water then plunging it into the ice water. Reserve the pot of boiling water. Remove the vegetables from the ice water, transfer them to a large bowl and toss them together.

Add lobsters, two at a time, to the pot of boiling water. Once the water returns to the boil, cook for 6 minutes. Remove lobsters from the water and plunge them into the ice bath. Repeat with the remaining two lobsters.

Lay the lobsters on their back. With a heavy chef's knife, cut the lobster tails from the bodies. Split the tails in half lengthwise, leaving the black roe attached, if you like. (You can also reserve the lobster roe for a lobster hollandaise; the roe will keep in an airtight container in the freezer for up to 1 month.) Remove and discard any viscera. The lobster meat should still be opaque in the centre.

On low heat, bring the nage to just below the simmering point. With the back of a knife or a nutcracker, crack open the lobster claws and the attached arms. Using tweezers or a lobster pick, remove the meat, trying not to break it apart. Add the lobster tails and the claw meat to the tarragon nage and poach for 2 minutes. The opaque flesh should become white and fully cooked and the roe (if you left it attached) will turn bright red. Transfer the lobster meat to a bowl.

Add the vegetables to the nage and cook until they are reheated. Season with salt and pepper and add a squeeze of lemon juice.

To serve Divide the vegetables equally among four large bowls. Arrange the lobster pieces on top of the vegetables and ladle the tarragon nage over each serving.

Suggested wine A good Côte de Beaune white, such as Meursault or Puligny Montrachet.

Grilled Lobsters

with Spicy Lobster Hollandaise

SERVES 4

Lobsters

- 4 Nova Scotia lobsters, 1½ lbs each
- 4 Tbsp butter
- 1 clove garlic, chopped
- 1 shallot, finely minced
- 1 cup toasted bread crumbs
- 2 Roma tomatoes, peeled, seeded and diced
- 4 sprigs parsley, leaves chopped
- ¼ cup grated Parmesan
- 4 Tbsp olive oil
- 1 lemon, in wedges

Hollandaise

- ¾ lb unsalted butter
- 2 egg yolks
- ¼ cup water
- Roe from 4 lobsters
- Dash of brandy
- 1 tsp cayenne pepper
- ½ lemon
- 1 tsp minced tarragon
- 1 tsp minced chervil
- ¼ tsp olive oil

Lobsters To make lobsters easier to handle, place them in the freezer for 15 minutes (this will cause them to fall into a dormant state) or boil them briefly in salted water for 1 minute then plunge them immediately into an ice bath.

Lay the lobsters on their back. With a heavy chef's knife, split the lobsters in half lengthwise. Turn the lobsters onto their belly with their heads pointing to the right (or, if you are left-handed, to the left). Place the tip of the knife in the centre of the head and pierce the shell, cutting between the antenna bases. Turn the lobster 180 degrees and cut through the rest of the head and right down to the tail. Separate the arms from the bodies and, with the back of a knife or with a nutcracker, crack the arms and the claws open. Using tweezers or a lobster pick, remove the meat, trying not to break it apart. Scrape out the innards from the head and intestines, reserving the greenish tomalley and the black roe. Pat the lobster halves dry with a paper towel and set aside.

In a small sauté pan, heat butter on medium-high heat until it browns, 1 to 4 minutes. Add garlic and shallot and cook for 30 seconds. Roughly chop the tomalley and add to the shallot mixture. Season with salt and pepper and cook for 2 minutes. Stir in bread crumbs, tomatoes, parsley and Parmesan and keep warm.

Hollandaise In a microwave-safe bowl, heat butter for 5 minutes in a microwave on high until the fat separates from the milk solids and water. Remove from the microwave and allow to rest for 10 minutes. Using a spoon, skim off and discard the top layer of foam. Slowly pour the fat into another bowl, being careful not to mix in any of the milk solids on the bottom. Discard the milk solids and set aside the clarified butter.

In a medium stainless-steel bowl, combine egg yolks with water. Place the bowl over a pot of gently simmering water and whisk the egg yolk mixture until it triples in volume and becomes thick and creamy, about 5 minutes. Slowly whisk in clarified butter until emulsified.

Place lobster roe and 1 Tbsp of water in a small food processor and purée until smooth. Strain the lobster purée through a fine-mesh sieve into a small saucepan.

Stir ¼ of the hollandaise into the lobster purée. Cook carefully over low heat, whisking constantly, until the mixture becomes bright red. Stir this red sauce into the remaining hollandaise. Add brandy, cayenne, a squeeze of lemon juice, tarragon, chervil and a pinch of salt and mix well. Set aside.

Preheat a grill to high. Lightly brush lobster claws with olive oil and season with salt. Grill for 3 minutes with the lid closed. While the claws are cooking, brush lobster halves with more olive oil. Turn the claws over and add the lobster halves, meat-side down. Close the lid and cook for 3 minutes, until char marks appear on the lobster tails. Move the claws to the top rack of the grill.

Turn the lobster halves onto the shell side. Spoon ⅛ of the tomalley–bread crumb stuffing into the head cavity of each lobster. Close the lid and cook for 2 minutes more. Remove lobster pieces from the grill and season the tails with salt.

To serve Arrange two lobster halves and a couple of claws per person on four plates. Serve with fresh lemon wedges and individual bowls of the lobster hollandaise.

Suggested wine This dish requires a bit of fruit to work with the spice; try a dry gewürztraminer from Alsace.

Littleneck Clams

with Linguine, Sea Asparagus and Pancetta

SERVES 4

- 8 cups water
- 4 oz sea asparagus, 1/2 inch removed from the bottoms
- 1/4 cup salt
- 10 oz linguine
- 2 Tbsp olive oil + extra for drizzling
- 2 1/2 oz pancetta, diced
- 2 cloves garlic, germ removed, thinly sliced on a mandolin
- 1/2 small onion, minced
- Pinch of hot red chili flakes
- 1 cup white wine
- 1/3 cup unsalted butter
- 2 lbs littleneck clams, thoroughly scrubbed and washed
- 1/2 cup chiffonaded Italian parsley
- 1/4 cup herbed bread crumbs (page 48)

Sea asparagus, also called samphire or Salicornia, is a grass-like sea vegetable that is salty and crunchy. It is available from specialty food stores from May through July.

Fill a large bowl with ice water. Bring a large pot of water to a boil on high heat. Add sea asparagus and blanch for 1 minute, then remove it from the water and plunge it into the ice bath to refresh.

Add salt to the same pot of water and cook linguine until it is al dente—oil is not necessary. Drain the linguine, reserving 1 cup of the starchy pasta water.

In a large sauté pan, heat olive oil on high heat. Add pancetta, garlic, onion and chili flakes and cook for 2 minutes until the mixture starts to brown. Add wine, butter and clams, then cover the pan and cook, shaking the pan regularly, until clams are open, 2 to 4 minutes. Discard any unopened clams.

Remove the clams from the pan and set them aside. Add linguine and reserved pasta water to the pan and toss in the clam juices. Add sea asparagus and swirl the pan for 1 minute over medium heat to emulsify all the juices and to coat the pasta evenly. Season with salt and pepper, then toss in the clams and parsley and a splash of fresh olive oil.

To serve Divide the pasta among four bowls and sprinkle with herbed bread crumbs.

Suggested wine A fruit-driven pinot blanc with good viscosity. Try something from Vouvray or the Willamette Valley.

Manila Clams Steamed

with Sake, Ginger and Ponzu

SERVES 4

- 3 lbs Manila clams, thoroughly washed
- 1/3 cup water
- 1 cup sake
- 2-inch piece of ginger, peeled and finely julienned
- 2 cloves garlic, thinly sliced
- 3 green onions, thinly sliced
- 1 1/2 oz fresh wakame seaweed, rinsed and coarsely chopped
- 2 Tbsp ponzu sauce
- 2 tsp mirin
- Pinch of shichimi togarashi (Japanese seven-spice seasoning)

In a large pot, combine clams and water. Cover the pot, bring to a boil on high heat, shaking it occasionally, and cook for 3 to 4 minutes, until clams have steamed open. Remove the clams with a slotted spoon and set them aside, discarding any unopened ones. (If you notice any strong-smelling clams among the open ones, discard the cooking liquid and replace it with sake.)

Strain the cooking liquid into a medium saucepan through a gold tea filter to remove any sand or shell pieces. Add sake, ginger and garlic and bring to a boil on high heat. Boil for 2 minutes, then add green onions, wakame, ponzu and mirin.

To serve Divide the clams among four bowls. Bring the sauce to a boil and pour it over the clams. For some heat, sprinkle the dish with togarashi.

Suggested wine A fresh Soave Classico from the Veneto region.

Cockle Clams

with Chorizo, Red Pepper, Fennel and Oregano

SERVES 4

- 4 Tbsp olive oil
- 2 oz panko (Japanese bread crumbs)
- 24 live cockle clams
- 1/2 cup white wine
- 1 small chorizo sausage, diced
- 1/4 small onion, minced
- 1 clove garlic, chopped
- 1/2 fennel bulb, diced
- 1 red bell pepper, seeded and diced
- Zest of 1/2 orange
- 1/2 lemon
- 1/4 cup fresh oregano leaves, roughly chopped
- 1/4 cup Italian parsley leaves, roughly chopped

Heat 2 Tbsp of olive oil in a sauté pan on medium heat. Add panko and cook for 2 minutes, until lightly toasted. Set aside.

In a large pot, combine clams and wine. Cook on high heat until the clams begin to open, 3 to 4 minutes. Remove the meat from the shells and refrigerate. Strain the cooking liquid through a gold tea filter and reserve. Rinse and reserve the clam shells, separating the shells at the hinges.

Take the clam meat out of the refrigerator. Cut off the tip of the siphon (the long neck) on each clam and remove the brown parts (gills and palps) between the siphon and the foot. Split the siphon open and rinse thoroughly under cold water to remove any sand. Rinse the foot as well.

Cut cleaned cockles into ¼-inch pieces.

In a small sauté pan, heat ½ tsp of the olive oil on high heat. Add chorizo and cook for about 1 minute. Don't overcook the sausage or it will dry out and become tough. Remove the sausage with a slotted spoon and allow it to drain on a paper towel. Reduce the heat to medium, discard half of the rendered fat, then add onion, garlic and fennel to the pan. Season with a pinch of salt and cook for 2 to 3 minutes until fragrant but not browned. Add red bell pepper and orange zest, season again with salt and pepper and continue cooking for 2 minutes. Deglaze the pan with the liquid reserved from cooking the cockle clams. Add a squeeze of lemon juice and remove the pan from the heat. Mix in cockle clam meat, chorizo, oregano, parsley and panko.

Preheat the oven to 350°F. Fill the clam half-shells with cockle mix and bake for 7 minutes.

To serve On each of four plates, arrange twelve half-shells.

Suggested wine A medium-bodied tempranillo offers good spices and dried fruit that pairs well with this dish.

Razor Clam Ceviche

with Kumquat, Celery, Coriander and Lime

SERVES 4

- 8 to 12 live razor clams
- 1 tsp salt
- 2 Tbsp finely sliced red onion
- Juice of 2 limes
- 1 small clove garlic, germ removed, julienned
- 1-inch piece of ginger, peeled and grated
- ½ red jalapeño pepper, seeded and julienned
- 4 kumquats, skin only, julienned
- Yellow rib of celery from the heart of the stalk, thinly sliced
- ¼ cup cilantro shoots or cilantro leaves, chiffonaded
- 2 cups canola oil, for deep-frying
- 1 cup cooked chickpeas
- Pinch of cayenne pepper

Razor clams are sweeter and meatier than other varieties of clams. They are usually available from October through May, either by harvesting them yourself or by buying them from good seafood stores.

Using a spoon, scrape the razor clam meat from the shells. Rinse the shells and set them aside.

Cut off the rubbery tip of the siphon (the long neck) with scissors and remove all of the visible brown parts (gills and palps) between the foot and the tube. Split the siphon open and rinse thoroughly in cold water to remove any sand. Split the foot open and quickly rinse to remove all the dark parts, being careful not to discard the soft and sweet white parts. With a sharp chef's knife, cut the razor clam meat into very thin strips. Set the meat aside in the refrigerator.

Rinse red onion under cold water for 2 minutes, then dry on a kitchen towel.

Season razor clam meat with the salt and marinate in a small bowl for 5 minutes with lime juice, garlic, red onion, ginger and jalapeño. Add kumquats, celery and cilantro and toss to combine.

Heat canola oil in a deep fryer to 350°F (use a thermometer to check the temperature). Add chickpeas and cook for 5 minutes, or until crisp and brown. Remove from the oil with a slotted spoon and drain on paper towels. Season with cayenne and a pinch of salt.

To serve Divide the chilled clam mixture among four chilled martini glasses. Serve fried chickpeas on the side.

Suggested wine Try a crisp riesling from Marlborough or the Clare Valley.

Savoury Clam and Corn Fritters

with Cumin-Tomato Sauce

SERVES 4

Fritters

- 2 lbs savoury clams
- 1/3 cup water
- 2 Tbsp olive oil
- 2 cloves garlic, chopped
- 1 red bell pepper, seeded and finely diced
- 1/2 cup corn kernels
- 1 Tbsp harissa
- 1/2 cup cilantro leaves, roughly chopped
- 1 bunch green onions, white and green parts, thinly sliced
- 1 1/2 cups all-purpose flour
- 1/4 cup cornmeal
- 1 tsp baking powder
- 1 tsp salt
- 2 eggs
- 1 1/4 cups milk
- 8 cups canola oil, for deep-frying

Cumin-tomato sauce

- 10 very ripe Roma tomatoes
- 1/2 cup ketchup
- 1 shallot, minced
- 1 red bell pepper, seeded and diced
- 1 tsp cumin seeds, toasted and crushed
- 1 tsp diced red jalapeño pepper
- 5 Tbsp olive oil
- 5 basil leaves, chiffonaded
- 12 Italian parsley leaves, chiffonaded

This recipe works just as well with littleneck clams. Harissa is a cumin-flavoured chili paste from Morocco; if you cannot find it at your local specialty food store, use chili purée instead.

Fritters In a large pot, combine clams and water. Cover the pot, bring to a boil on high heat, shaking it occasionally, and cook for 3 to 4 minutes, until clams have steamed open. Remove the clams with a slotted spoon and set them aside, discarding any unopened ones. Take the clam meat out of the shells and set it aside in a bowl.

In a medium sauté pan, heat olive oil on high heat. Add garlic, red bell pepper and corn kernels and cook for 1 minute. Season with salt and pepper. Stir in harissa, cilantro, green onions and clam meat. Set aside to cool.

In a medium bowl, mix together flour, cornmeal, baking powder and salt. In another bowl, whisk together eggs and milk. Stir dry ingredients into wet ingredients until well combined. Fold in the clam mixture.

Heat canola oil in a deep fryer or a deep pot to 350°F (check the temperature with a deep-fat thermometer). Fry spoonfuls of batter in the oil until cooked and golden brown, about 3 minutes per batch. Remove the fritters from the oil with a slotted spoon and allow them to drain on a paper towel. (You will have about 40 fritters.) When the fritters have cooled slightly, taste and season if necessary.

Cumin-tomato sauce Fill a large bowl with ice water. Bring a large pot of water to a boil. Add tomatoes and blanch for 30 seconds, then plunge them into the ice bath. Peel and seed the tomatoes.

In a blender or food processor, blend tomatoes, ketchup, shallot, red bell pepper, cumin seeds, jalapeño and olive oil. Season with salt and pepper, then stir in basil and parsley.

To serve Arrange the fritters in a large serving bowl. Pour the sauce into a smaller serving bowl. Set an empty plate in front of each guest and pass around the fritters and cumin-tomato sauce, so guests can serve themselves, family style.

Suggested wine Try a light red like a Cannonau di Sardegna.

Honey Mussels in Mild Garlic Cream

with Roasted Red Pepper Jelly and Pine Nuts

SERVES 4

Mussels

- 24 large Honey Mussels
- 1/2 cup white wine
- 30 cloves garlic, germs removed
- 4 Tbsp unsalted butter
- 1 small white onion, minced
- 1 leek, white part only, in thin rings
- 1 sprig thyme
- 1 bay leaf
- 2 cups chicken stock (page 184)
- 1 small potato, peeled and diced
- 1 cup whipping cream
- 4 Tbsp red pepper jelly (page 80)
- 1 Tbsp pine nuts, toasted

Parmesan brittle

- 2 oz grated Parmesan (about 4 Tbsp)

Mussels Combine mussels and wine in a large pot. Cover, and cook on high heat for 2 to 3 minutes until mussels start to open. Remove the ones that open immediately so they do not become overcooked, and discard any mussels that do not open after 3 minutes. Extract the mussel meat, setting it aside in a bowl, and discard the shells. Strain the cooking liquid through a gold tea filter to remove any sand and shell pieces.

In a small pot, cover garlic with cold water and bring it to a boil on high heat. Drain and repeat twice.

In a large sauté pan, heat butter on medium heat. Add onion, leek, garlic and a pinch of salt and sauté until soft but not browned, about 5 minutes. Add the cooking liquid from the mussels, thyme and bay leaf. Cook until liquid has reduced by two-thirds, about 3 minutes. Add chicken stock and potato and simmer until potatoes are well cooked, about 15 minutes. Remove thyme and bay leaf, add cream and bring the mixture to a boil. Remove from the heat, allow this mixture to cool for 5 minutes, then purée for 1 minute in a blender. Pass the garlic cream through a fine-mesh sieve into a bowl and season with salt and pepper.

Parmesan brittle Preheat the oven to 350°F. Line a baking sheet with a silicone mat. Spoon 1 Tbsp of cheese onto the mat. Shape the cheese into a 2-inch circle. Repeat, making four circles 2 inches apart. Bake for 3 to 5 minutes, until the cheese is bubbly and the edges begin to colour. Slide the silicone mat off the hot baking sheet onto a clean plate and allow the brittles to cool for 1 minute. Remove them with a small spatula. Roughly crumble the brittles.

To serve In each of four soup bowls, spoon one-quarter cup of the garlic cream. Arrange a quarter of the mussels in the garlic cream. Arrange a tablespoon of red pepper jelly in each bowl and sprinkle with pine nuts. Garnish each serving with pieces of Parmesan brittle.

Suggested wine A rich and complex Bandol Rosé.

Honey Mussels in Brick Sheets

with Shiso Leaves

SERVES 4

- 1/3 cup soy sauce
- 3/4 cup water
- 3 leaves gelatin, softened in a little cold water
- 2 Tbsp sake
- 2 Tbsp mirin
- 24 large B.C. Honey Mussels, scrubbed and debearded
- 8 Tbsp shiro miso (white miso paste)
- 1 Tbsp Dijon mustard
- 1 Tbsp yuzu juice
- 16 shiso leaves, 12 of them halved and 4 of them chiffonaded
- 24 squares Moroccan brick dough, each 4 inches
- 1 egg white, lightly beaten
- 1 Tbsp extra-virgin olive oil
- Pinch of fleur de sel
- 8 scallions, white part only, sliced
- 1/2 tsp espelette pepper, for garnish
- 1/2 tsp powdered yuzu rind, for garnish

Yuzu rind, like yuzu juice, mirin, shiro miso and shiso leaves (also known as perilla leaves), is available at Asian supermarkets. Sheets of brick dough can be purchased at North African or specialty food stores. If you cannot find them, use spring roll wrappers instead.

In a medium bowl, combine soy sauce and water. Transfer a quarter of this mixture to a small saucepan and heat on medium heat. Press out the moisture from the gelatin leaves, then dissolve them in the warm soy sauce. Combine this mixture with the rest of the soy sauce, then whip it with a hand-held blender for about 2 minutes until it is light and airy. Pour this mixture into a whipped cream dispenser and charge with one cartridge of nitrous oxide. Refrigerate until cold, about 1 hour.

While the foam is chilling, preheat the oven to 350°F.

Fill a bowl with cold water. Combine sake and mirin in a medium saucepan. Add mussels and heat on high heat until mussels have steamed open, 2 to 3 minutes. Remove the mussels with a slotted spoon and plunge them into the cold water. Set aside.

Strain cooking liquid through a gold tea filter into a small bowl. Add shiro miso, Dijon mustard and yuzu juice and whisk to combine.

Take the mussels out of their shells and pat them dry with a kitchen towel. Discard the shells. Locate the opening in each cooked mussel, then fill it with ½ tsp of the miso mixture. Wrap the mussel first in half a shiso leaf, then roll it in a square of brick dough and dab the end with a little egg white to seal the roll. Lightly brush each roll with olive oil, place on a baking sheet and bake for 1 minute, until the outside is golden. Remove from the heat and set aside.

In a small dish, combine extra-virgin olive oil and fleur de sel. Add scallions and marinate for 5 minutes.

To serve Remove the canister from the refrigerator and shake well for a minute. On each of four rectangular plates, spray six dots of the soy mixture in a line. Lay one scallion slice beside each dot and sprinkle the shiso chiffonade along this line. Place one mussel bonbon beside each scallion slice. Garnish each plate with a dusting of espelette pepper and powdered yuzu rind.

Suggested wine Try a fruit-driven pinot blanc with good viscosity, such as one from Vouvray or the Willamette Valley.

Four Sauces for Raw Oysters

on the Half Shell

SERVES 4

Granité of cherry mignonette

- 5 oz pitted cherries
- 1 cup aged red wine vinegar
- Pinch of brown sugar
- 4 shallots, minced
- 1 tsp coarsely ground pepper + extra for garnish
- 1 Tbsp fresh thyme leaves + extra for garnish

Kombu and sake mignonette

- 5 Tbsp sake
- 1-inch piece of kombu seaweed
- 5 Tbsp rice vinegar
- 1 Tbsp mirin
- Pinch of grated fresh ginger
- 2 Tbsp finely diced cucumber
- 2 shiso leaves, thinly sliced

Spicy ponzu sauce

- 1/4 cup ponzu sauce (or 2 Tbsp orange juice, 1 Tbsp lemon juice and 1 Tbsp lime juice)
- 3 Tbsp soy sauce
- 1 Tbsp shredded daikon radish
- Dash of Japanese chili sauce
- 1 green onion, thinly sliced

Creamy sesame sauce

- 1/3 cup mayonnaise
- 2 Tbsp sesame oil
- 2 Tbsp rice vinegar
- 2 Tbsp yuzu juice
- 2 Tbsp soy sauce
- 1 Tbsp black sesame seeds

Kombu is a black seaweed that tastes briny like the ocean. Here it is paired with sake that has been boiled to eliminate its alcoholic flavour. Japanese chili sauce has a unique taste that is not quite replicated by other chili sauces.

Granité of cherry mignonette
In a food processor, purée cherries with vinegar and sugar and strain the mixture through a fine-mesh sieve into a bowl. Add a pinch of salt, shallots, pepper and thyme and allow to infuse for 2 days.

Strain and pour the infusion into a deep-sided dish, then place the dish in the freezer. Stir the mixture with a fork about once every 15 minutes to break up the ice sheet. Once the granité has crystallized (usually after about 2 hours), transfer it to a small container and store it in the freezer until ready to serve.

Kombu and sake mignonette In a small saucepan, bring sake and kombu to a boil on high heat. Cook for 2 minutes, then remove from the heat. Remove kombu from the sake and dice finely. Refrigerate the sake until it is cool, about 10 minutes. In a small bowl, combine kombu, sake, vinegar, mirin, ginger, cucumber and shiso until well mixed.

Spicy ponzu sauce Combine all ingredients in a small bowl and stir to mix.

Creamy sesame sauce Combine all ingredients in a small bowl and stir to mix.

To serve Shuck 24 to 48 oysters and arrange them on a platter of ice. Allow guests to spoon the desired sauce onto each oyster. For oysters topped with the granité of cherry mignonette, garnish with freshly ground black pepper and a few thyme leaves before serving.

Suggested wine A non-vintage citrus Champagne.

Pacific Oysters

Baked with Pernod, Orange and Fennel

SERVES 4

- 12 medium Pacific oysters
- 3 Tbsp olive oil
- ½ cup diced fennel
- 2 shallots, finely diced
- 1 clove garlic, germ removed, finely chopped
- 7 oz baby spinach leaves
- 4 egg yolks
- 2 Tbsp Pernod
- 2 Tbsp cold water
- 3 Tbsp unsalted butter
- Pinch of coarse sea salt
- Pinch of cayenne pepper
- 1 lemon, halved
- ¼ cup dry bread crumbs
- Zest of ½ orange
- 1 Tbsp fresh thyme leaves
- 2 lbs rock salt for baking the oysters
- 1½ oz dried wakame seaweed
- 1 Tbsp coriander seeds
- 1 Tbsp fennel seeds
- 1 Tbsp lemon peel

Shuck the oysters, keeping the bottom shell and reserving the oyster liquor. Remove all of the bits of shell from the oyster.

In a medium sauté pan, heat 2 Tbsp of the olive oil on medium heat. Add fennel, shallots and garlic and cook for 2 minutes. Season with salt and pepper, then add baby spinach and cook until wilted, 30 to 60 seconds. Drain the spinach and vegetables on a kitchen towel.

In a medium stainless-steel bowl, combine egg yolks, Pernod, cold water and the oyster liquor. Place the bowl over a pot of gently simmering water and whisk the egg yolk mixture until it becomes very airy and thickens to the point where you can write an 8 on its surface. Add butter to stabilize this sabayon and season with sea salt, cayenne and a squeeze of lemon juice, being careful not to disturb the air in the sabayon.

Heat 1 Tbsp of olive oil in a sauté pan on medium heat. Add bread crumbs and toast for 1 minute until golden brown. Add orange zest and thyme leaves and season with salt and pepper.

Preheat the oven to 425°F. Combine rock salt, wakame, coriander seeds, fennel seeds and lemon peel and spread on a baking sheet. Arrange the empty oyster half-shells on the salt. Fill the shells with the spinach mixture, place oysters on top, sprinkle them with the bread crumb mix and squeeze lemon juice on each oyster. Spoon the sabayon on the oysters and bake for 10 minutes until the sabayon is golden brown and the oysters are warmed through.

To serve Arrange a small amount of the warm rock salt mixture on each of four plates. Divide the baked oysters among the plates and serve immediately.

Suggested wine Try a good prosecco or cava.

Kusshi Oysters

with Pickled Vegetables, Cucumber Jelly and Horseradish Foam

SERVES 4

Kusshi oysters are an extra-small, meaty variety of oyster. To make the horseradish foam, you will need a whipped cream dispenser, which can be found at kitchen supply stores.

Horseradish foam Place horseradish in a heatproof bowl. In a small saucepan, bring water and cream to a boil and pour over horseradish.

Press out the moisture from the gelatin leaf. Dissolve gelatin in the warm horseradish cream, then strain through a fine-mesh sieve into a bowl. Add lemon juice, sugar and a couple of pinches of salt. Pour this horseradish cream into the whipped cream dispenser and charge the dispenser with one cartridge of nitrous oxide. Keep the dispenser refrigerated for 2 hours until ready to serve.

Cucumber jelly Combine cucumber with sea salt. Allow to stand for 10 minutes and press the juice through a fine-mesh sieve into a heatproof bowl. (You should have about 1 cup of cucumber juice.) Warm 2 Tbsp of the cucumber juice in the microwave for 15 seconds. Press out the excess moisture from the gelatin, then dissolve it in the warm cucumber juice. Pour this mixture into the remaining cucumber juice and mix thoroughly.

Line an 8-inch × 14-inch deep-sided baking sheet with plastic wrap. Pour the cucumber mixture onto the baking sheet, then refrigerate for 2 hours until the jelly has completely set. Using a round cutter 1½ inches in diameter, cut out 12 disks.

Pickled vegetables In a medium heatproof bowl, mix together red onion, fennel, celery and cucumber.

In a saucepan, combine vinegar, mirin, chili flakes, thyme, ginger, coriander seeds and peppercorns. Bring to a boil on high heat, then remove from the heat and refrigerate until chilled.

Strain the vinegar mixture over the vegetables. Cover the bowl with plastic wrap and refrigerate for 1 hour.

To serve Shuck the oysters. Strain the pickled vegetables and mix them in a small bowl with the chopped chives. On each of four chilled rectangular plates, arrange a line of three small nests of pickled vegetables. Place a shucked oyster on each of the nests and top each serving with a disc of cucumber jelly. Carefully spray a small amount of horseradish foam between the nests and garnish with the chive tops.

Suggested wine Chablis with good minerality and stone fruit. Try a Grand Cru Les Clos.

Horseradish foam

- ½ cup fresh grated horseradish
- ½ cup water
- ½ cup whipping cream
- 1 leaf gelatin, softened in a little cold water
- 1 Tbsp lemon juice
- Pinch of sugar

Cucumber jelly

- 1 English cucumber, grated
- 1 tsp coarse sea salt
- 4 leaves gelatin, softened in a little cold water

Pickled vegetables

- ¼ red onion, julienned
- ¼ bulb fennel, julienned
- 2 ribs celery, julienned (about ½ cup)
- ½ cucumber, julienned (about ½ cup)
- 1 cup rice wine vinegar
- ½ cup mirin
- Pinch of hot red chili flakes
- 2 sprigs thyme
- 2 thin slices fresh ginger
- 1 tsp coriander seeds
- 1 tsp black peppercorns
- 1 Tbsp chopped chives, chopped + chive tops for garnish

12 small kusshi oysters

Pink Swimming Scallops

with Tomato-Lemon Compote

SERVES 4

- 28 fresh pink swimming scallops
- 12 Roma tomatoes
- 1/4 cup olive oil
- 2 shallots, sliced
- 1 clove garlic, sliced
- Zest of 1 lemon
- 1 Tbsp chopped capers
- 2 Tbsp chopped parsley
- Pinch of sugar
- 2 Tbsp butter
- 3/4 cup dry bread crumbs
- 1 Tbsp thyme leaves

Shuck scallops, keeping bottom shells and discarding top shells. Remove the beard and dirt sack from each scallop, but leave the scallop muscle and roe intact. Fill a pot with salted water, add scallops and allow to rinse for 5 minutes.

Fill a bowl with ice water. Bring a medium pot of water to a boil on high heat. Add tomatoes and blanch for 10 seconds, then plunge them into the ice bath. Peel and seed the tomatoes, then dice the flesh.

In a medium sauté pan, heat olive oil on medium heat. Add shallots and garlic and cook until fragrant, about 1 minute. Add tomatoes and lemon zest, then reduce the heat to low and cook until tomato water has evaporated, about 30 minutes. Remove from the heat, add capers, parsley and sugar, then season with salt and pepper.

Melt butter in a sauté pan on medium heat. Add bread crumbs and cook for 1 minute, or until golden brown. Add thyme leaves and mix well to combine.

Turn the broiler on. Place the scallop shells on a baking sheet, then onto each scallop shell, spoon 1 tsp of the tomato-lemon compote. Top with a scallop, then sprinkle the scallops with the bread crumb mixture. Broil for 3 to 4 minutes, until bread crumbs are golden and the scallops are cooked.

To serve Divide the scallops evenly among four plates.

Suggested wine This dish would be best with a crisp bubble; try something from the Okanagan.

Green Pea and Butter Lettuce Soup

with Swimming Scallops, Bacon and Croutons

SERVES 4

Chive cream In a small bowl, combine whipped cream, lime zest, lemon zest, orange zest and chives. Cover with plastic wrap and refrigerate until needed.

Pea and lettuce soup In a large pot, melt butter on medium heat. Add leek, onion and garlic and sweat for 5 minutes, then season with salt and pepper. Add chicken stock and bouquet garni and cook for 10 minutes. Add fresh green peas and butter lettuce and cook for 5 minutes until peas are cooked, then add frozen peas and remove the pot from the heat. Discard the bouquet garni. Immediately, transfer the soup to a blender or a food processor (working in batches, if necessary) and purée for 2 minutes to obtain a fine soup. Strain the soup through a medium-mesh sieve and season with salt and pepper.

In a medium pot, combine scallops and water. Cook on high heat until scallops begin to open, 2 to 3 minutes. Remove from the heat, drain, then extract scallop muscle meat and scallop roe. Discard the rest of the scallops.

In a medium sauté pan, toss together bread and 2 Tbsp of the olive oil on medium heat until golden and crispy, 2 to 3 minutes. Remove the croutons from the pan and allow them to drain on a kitchen towel.

In the sauté pan, heat the remaining 2 Tbsp of olive oil on high heat. Add bacon and cook for 2 minutes, then add scallop meat and roe and toss briefly. Season with salt and pepper, then add green onion, parsley and croutons. Toss again to mix.

To serve Divide bacon, scallops and croutons among four soup bowls. Serve soup from a tureen at the table and garnish each bowl with a quarter of the chive cream.

Suggested wine An aromatic gewürztraminer from the Okanagan would work well, but if you're adventurous, try a medium-sweet Vermouth served slightly chilled.

Chive cream

- 1 cup whipped cream
- Zest of 1/2 lime
- Zest of 1/2 lemon
- Zest of 1/4 orange
- 2 Tbsp minced chives

Pea and lettuce soup

- 1/4 cup unsalted butter
- 1 small leek, white and light green parts, thinly sliced
- 1/2 small onion, thinly sliced
- 3 cloves garlic, coarsely chopped
- 4 cups chicken stock (page 184)
- 2 sprigs thyme, 2 sprigs parsley and 1 sprig tarragon, tied into a bouquet garni
- 18 oz freshly shucked green peas
- 2 heads of butter lettuce, washed and chopped
- 9 oz frozen green peas
- 1 lb swimming scallops (about 24 scallops)
- 1/4 cup water
- 2 slices white bread, crusts removed, diced
- 4 Tbsp olive oil
- 3 oz smoked bacon, diced
- 1 green onion, white and green parts, thinly sliced
- 1 Tbsp chiffonaded Italian parsley

Sesame-crusted Weathervane Scallops

with Japanese Eggplant

SERVES 4

Spicy yuzu vinaigrette

- 3 Tbsp olive oil
- 3 Tbsp grapeseed oil
- 2 Tbsp yuzu juice
- 2 Tbsp soy sauce
- 1 bird's eye chili pepper, seeded and finely chopped
- ½ clove garlic, finely chopped
- 2 green onions, thinly sliced
- 1 tsp freshly grated ginger
- 10 Italian parsley leaves, chiffonaded
- 3 shiso leaves, chiffonaded

Eggplant

- 2 small Japanese eggplants, halved lengthwise
- 2 Tbsp sesame oil

Shiro miso sauce

- 3 Tbsp sake
- 3 Tbsp mirin
- ¼ cup shiro miso (white miso paste)
- 1 egg yolk

Scallops

- 16 medium weathervane scallops
- 4 Tbsp grapeseed oil
- 2 Tbsp black sesame seeds
- 2 Tbsp white sesame seeds, toasted

Bird's eye chilies are very small, very hot peppers. If you can't find them, use a quarter of a jalapeño pepper.

Spicy yuzu vinaigrette In a small bowl, whisk together olive oil, grapeseed oil, yuzu juice, soy sauce, bird's eye chili and garlic. Stir in green onions, ginger, parsley and shiso with a spoon. Season with some salt, if necessary.

Eggplant Turn the broiler on. Cut a criss-cross pattern on the cut side of the eggplant, brush with sesame oil and season lightly with salt. Place eggplants, cut-side up, on a baking sheet and broil for 10 minutes until soft and lightly browned.

Shiro miso sauce In a small saucepan, bring sake and mirin to a boil on high heat. Boil for 20 seconds, reduce the heat to low, add shiro miso and cook, stirring constantly with a wooden spoon, until the mixture becomes creamy and slightly thickened, about 2 minutes. Mix in egg yolk and cook for another 2 minutes. Remove from the heat.

Scallops Pat scallops dry with a kitchen towel, and keep them at room temperature.

Heat a large sauté pan over very high heat for 1 minute until a drop of water dripped into the pan evaporates immediately. Add 2 Tbsp of the grapeseed oil and place half of the scallops in the oil. (Cooking the scallops in two batches will prevent overcrowding, which will boil rather than sear the scallops.) Sear the scallops on each side for 45 seconds or until you can see the edges becoming golden brown—in total no more than 1 to 2 minutes. Flip them and place them quickly onto a kitchen towel. Season with salt and pepper.

Quickly wash the pan and repeat with the other half of the scallops.

To serve Turn the broiler on. Spread two tablespoons of the shiro miso sauce on the eggplant and broil again until the miso sauce starts to brown, about two minutes.

Mix together the black and white sesame seeds. Brush one side of each scallop with the miso sauce and dip it in the sesame seeds. Place four scallops, sesame-side up, on each of four plates. Arrange half of a broiled eggplant on each plate then drizzle with the spicy yuzu vinaigrette.

Suggested wine Try a good German riesling, kabinett level.

Qualicum Beach Scallops

with Garam Masala, Candied Ginger Sauce and Citrus Relish

SERVES 4

Garam masala

- 2 Tbsp cumin seeds
- 2 Tbsp coriander seeds
- 2 Tbsp cardamom seeds
- 2 Tbsp black peppercorns
- 1 tsp whole cloves
- 1 tsp fresh grated nutmeg
- 1 tsp turmeric
- 1 tsp hot red chili flakes

Citrus relish

- 1 Tbsp grapeseed oil
- 1 shallot, finely minced
- 1 tsp chopped fresh ginger
- ½ red bell pepper, seeded and finely diced
- ½ small red jalapeño pepper, seeded and diced
- 1 lime, peeled, sectioned and membranes discarded
- 1 pink grapefruit, peeled and sectioned
- 1 orange, peeled and sectioned
- 1 lemon, peeled and sectioned
- 1 Tbsp thinly sliced crystallized ginger
- ¼ cup fresh cilantro leaves, chiffonaded

The spiciness of the scallops in this dish is elevated with a sauce made from preserved ginger in syrup, not to be confused with Japanese pickled ginger. Preserved ginger is available at specialty food stores.

Garam masala Combine cumin seeds, coriander seeds, cardamom, peppercorns and cloves in a dry, heavy skillet on medium-high heat. Toast the spices, stirring occasionally, until they darken and give off a sweet smoky aroma, about 10 minutes. Allow to cool completely.

In a clean coffee or spice grinder, combine all of the toasted spices, nutmeg, turmeric and chili flakes and grind them to a fine powder. Pass the mixture through a medium-mesh sieve into a small bowl. Will keep in an airtight container at room temperature for up to 2 weeks.

Citrus relish In a large sauté pan, heat grapeseed oil on high heat. Add shallot, fresh ginger, red bell pepper and jalapeño and sauté for 2 minutes. Season with salt and pepper and set aside to cool. Stir in lime, grapefruit, orange, lemon, crystallized ginger and cilantro and reserve at room temperature. Will keep refrigerated in an airtight container for up to 1 week.

Ginger sauce In a small bowl, blend preserved and grated ginger into warm white wine sauce. Strain through a medium-mesh sieve into a clean bowl, then season with salt, pepper and lime juice.

Ginger sauce

- 2 pieces preserved ginger without the syrup
- Pinch of freshly grated ginger
- 1/2 cup white wine sauce (page 188), warmed
- Juice of 1/2 lime

Scallops

- 16 medium Qualicum Beach scallops, dried with a kitchen towel
- 4 Tbsp garam masala
- 4 Tbsp grapeseed oil

Scallops Season scallops with salt and garam masala. Heat grapeseed oil in a large sauté pan on high heat and add half of the scallops, searing them until the edges start to become crispy and the insides are just warm, 45 seconds to 1 minute per side. (Cooking the scallops in two batches will prevent overcrowding, which will boil rather than sear the scallops.) Repeat with the other half of the scallops.

To serve Using a hand-held blender, froth the ginger sauce for one minute. Arrange four scallops on each of four individual plates and dab some of the citrus relish among the scallops. Spoon the ginger sauce around the dish.

Suggested wine An off-dry riesling from Mosel, spätlese level.

UNSUNG HEROES

UNSUNG HEROES

THE APPROACH is simple: conserve overused, underpopulated species of fish and shellfish by using underused, abundant species. However, the matter of preparing these species in ways that will attract and even educate people to explore and expand their seafood palate is not as simple. Frank Pabst does not hesitate when asked about this approach. "It is a crusade, actually," he says. In many cases, the situation is dire. The Cousteau Society internationally, the David Suzuki Foundation closer to home and various established Pacific Coast aquariums all agree. And while nearly 90 per cent of the world's large fish population is extinct and while current fish and shellfish populations across the world are a relatively small fraction of past levels, quota systems, stricter regulations on bycatches and increased commercial interest in much more plentiful species can effect positive change.

Frank decided to lead, not follow. He instituted at Blue Water Cafe what he not so fancifully calls "Unsung Heroes." It is a special menu offered for one month, early each year. Underappreciated species are the cornerstone of this menu. In other parts of the world, some of these species—notably herring, sardines and mackerel—are not at all underappreciated, but in the Pacific Northwest, with its previously bountiful and relatively easily accessible salmon, halibut and shellfish, diners' palates are generally attuned to these somewhat less intense flavours from the ocean.

Frank says, "The Unsung Heroes are usually what we think of as 'fishy fish.'" Hence the real genius of his program: he applies his creative technique to making dishes that showcase these strong-flavoured fish, in preparations that actually use the bolder flavours in dishes that complement them, round them out and make them, in essence, approachable and delectable. As a result, people's minds begin to change as they realize how extremely delicious the simple sardine, the tiny periwinkle or the common barnacle can be.

Mackerel possess perhaps the epitome of that pronounced strong fish flavour that Frank talks about. Unlike the tuna, a close cousin, mackerel found in the Pacific Ocean are quite small and have an intense flavour. The fishery is regulated, and its season in Canada is May through November. Adding to the sometimes overwhelming flavour is the fact that this fish deteriorates more rapidly than most after the catch, so anything less than sterling freshness creates a noticeable problem. At Blue Water Cafe, that issue is never, so to speak, on the table, and the flavours are vivid, never "fishy."

Sardines caught and served fresh are completely different from the tinned product so many Canadians know and tend to love or hate. Fresh sardines at Blue Water Cafe, served various ways but always showcasing the firm texture and surprisingly mild flavour of the dark meat, are a revelation—a testimonial to wise, sustainable, delicious alternatives.

Herring from Pacific coastal waters have been spoken for by the Japanese market for many decades, for processing into canned products but also, notably, for the delicacy known as herring spawn-on-kelp. Any fishery that targets a species' spawn in great numbers will have sustainability issues, as one would expect, and indeed, the Pacific spawn-on-kelp fishery is in dire condition. It is available only in March and April of each year. Fresh herring, however, sometimes offered sashimi-style at Blue Water Cafe, are remarkable fish with deep, rich flavour and a lovely meaty texture. Herring are a true discovery for the home cook, especially after being inspired by a dish at Blue Water Cafe.

Sea urchins seem an unlikely species for fine dining, but in fact these creatures offer up a succulent meat that can accommodate a variety of preparations. Green, black and sometimes red, these creatures, which have been around for more than 500 million years, are also prized for their roe, known as *uni* in the Japanese market, where it is considered a delicacy. September through April is the catch season.

Squid are known more commonly as calamari and are susceptible to a certain prejudice because of poor preparations that commonly render it overcooked and rubbery. Squid is in fact a marvellous and versatile food. At Blue Water Cafe, it might be paired with Dungeness crab on a bed of couscous, green onions and chickpeas. Neon flying squid in the Pacific Ocean are highly migratory, available only from July through early October. Native to Chile, the much larger Humboldt squid were introduced to Pacific coastal waters only recently, thanks to El Niño.

Octopus are a great sustainable seafood choice, particularly because, owing to the particular traps used to catch them, their bycatch quotient is very low. They tend to live on the eastern side of Vancouver Island, from Port Hardy south to Sooke. Their meat is fairly mild, considering they are fearsome predators in their habitat. Octopus are an increasingly hot commodity for chefs, who love their versatility.

Cuttlefish are not fish but molluscs, related to squid and octopus. They are found in shallow, sandy, warmer Pacific waters and range in size from two inches to nearly six feet. While it may be easy to imagine preparations that would flatter this species based on experience with the more commonly available squid, its flavour profile is richer and its texture more delicate, and some good working knowledge is required to prepare cuttlefish. The dark ink of cuttlefish is also often used in dishes.

Periwinkle, a type of sea snail, well deserve their fanciful name. These molluscs are tiny, but, cooked fresh and usually plucked out of their shell to eat, they pack a delectable punch. They are often used as an accompaniment to another component on a plate or even as an *amuse bouche*, simply adorned.

Gooseneck barnacles, a delicacy in Spain and Portugal and among First Nations peoples along the Pacific Coast, are now gaining acceptance on a wider scale. Goosenecks live in the intertidal zone, and their harvest is limited to Clayoquot and Barclay sounds. They are also difficult to harvest; the harvester's tool of choice is a special crowbar. Although Europeans consider barnacles fine on their own with just a little boiling in water to reduce salinity, at Blue Water Cafe these humble creatures attain great heights in a variety of preparations.

Jellyfish contain high levels of collagen and as such have been used in most of Asia for centuries as a treatment for ailments such as arthritis and high blood pressure. Although they are basically flavourless on their own, jellyfish add a fascinating textural component to vegetable dishes and salads.

Seaweed—how humble can it get? This marine plant is so common many people do not even notice it around them. Seaweed, in its many different varieties, is almost like coffee, tea or wine, in terms of its varied flavours, textures and appearance. At Blue Water Cafe, from the Raw Bar to main-room tables, it adorns and accompanies other components and in some ways is the ultimate example of an "unsung hero."

Mackerel

with Sweet and Sour Eggplant, Butternut Squash, Pine Nuts and Capers

SERVES 4

- 1/2 cup extra-virgin olive oil
- 4 Japanese eggplants, diced
- 5 oz butternut squash, diced (about 1 cup)
- 2 ribs celery, diced
- 1/4 red onion, thinly sliced (about 1/2 cup)
- 2 cloves garlic, chopped
- 1/4 cup red wine vinegar
- 1 Tbsp sugar
- 1 Tbsp capers, rinsed and coarsely chopped
- Zest of 1/2 lemon
- 1/8 cup chopped parsley
- 1/8 cup chopped basil
- 4 mackerel fillets, each 4 1/2 oz, skin on and deboned
- 1/2 lemon
- 1 Tbsp pine nuts, toasted

In a medium sauté pan, heat 3 Tbsp of the olive oil on medium heat. Add eggplants and sauté until cooked and lightly browned, 3 to 4 minutes. Remove the eggplants from the pan and set them aside to cool. Repeat with squash, cooking 3 to 4 minutes until done.

Heat 2 Tbsp of the olive oil on medium heat in a medium sauté pan. Add celery, red onion and garlic and sauté until just about done, 3 to 4 minutes. Season with salt and pepper, then add vinegar, sugar, capers and lemon zest. Allow to simmer for a couple of minutes, then set aside to cool.

In a medium bowl, combine the eggplant, squash and celery mixture. Add parsley and basil and 2 Tbsp of the olive oil. Refrigerate if you would like to serve this salad cold. It can also be enjoyed at room temperature.

Season the mackerel fillets with salt and pepper. In a medium sauté pan, heat 1 Tbsp of the olive oil on high heat. Add mackerel, skin-side down, and pan-fry for 1 minute, then turn the fish over and cook for 30 seconds more.

To serve On each of four plates, heap a quarter of the eggplant mixture. Top with a mackerel fillet. Finish the dish with a sprinkling of coarse sea salt and a squeeze of fresh lemon juice. Sprinkle with the pine nuts.

Suggested wine Try a light and fresh grüner veltliner from Austria.

Grilled Mackerel

with Chunky Romesco Sauce and Scallions

SERVES 4

The romesco sauce is best made the day before you plan to serve it.

Romesco sauce Preheat a grill to high. Place red bell peppers directly on the grill and cook, turning occasionally, until the skins are lightly charred on all sides. Remove from the heat, place in a covered bowl and allow to cool. Using a sharp knife, remove and discard the peel and seeds, then finely chop bell peppers.

Fill a bowl with ice water. Bring a small pot of water to a boil on high heat. Add tomatoes and blanch for 10 seconds, then plunge them into the ice bath. Peel the tomatoes, cut them in half and discard the seeds, then cut into a small dice.

Preheat the oven to 375°F. Place almonds and hazelnuts on a baking sheet and toast nuts for 4 minutes. Remove from the oven, allow to cool, then rub the nuts with a kitchen towel to remove the loose skins. Roughly chop the nuts.

Heat olive oil in a small sauté pan on medium heat. Add bread crumbs and garlic and toast until golden and crispy, about 2 minutes. Add chopped nuts, red bell peppers, tomatoes, shallot and vinegar. Season with paprika, salt and espelette pepper, then cook for 10 minutes, stirring frequently. Remove from the heat and allow to cool slightly.

In a blender or a food processor, purée ⅓ of this mixture. Stir this purée back into the sauce. Add parsley and set aside to cool.

Grilled mackerel Preheat a grill to high. Brush mackerel with ½ Tbsp olive oil, season with salt and pepper and grill, skin-side down, for 2 minutes. Turn the fish over and grill for 30 seconds more. Transfer fish to a plate and squeeze with fresh lemon juice.

Brush green onions with ½ Tbsp olive oil and grill until lightly browned. Season with salt and pepper.

Heat 2 Tbsp of olive oil in a sauté pan on medium heat. Add focaccia slices and pan-fry on both sides until golden brown and crunchy, about 2 minutes. Drain on paper towels to absorb the excess moisture, then rub croutons with garlic.

To serve Place a mackerel fillet on each plate. Arrange a slice of focaccia beside the fish. Top the focaccia with two tablespoons of romesco sauce and two green onions.

Suggested wine Try a light and fresh grüner veltliner from Austria.

Romesco sauce

- 4 red bell peppers
- 2 ripe Roma tomatoes
- 1 oz raw almonds
- 1 oz raw hazelnuts
- 2 Tbsp extra-virgin olive oil
- 2 Tbsp focaccia bread crumbs
- 3 cloves garlic, minced
- 1 shallot, minced
- 3 Tbsp aged sherry vinegar
- 1 Tbsp Spanish paprika
- 1 tsp espelette pepper
- Handful of fresh flat-leaf parsley, roughly chopped

Grilled mackerel

- 4 mackerel fillets, each 4½ oz, skin on but deboned
- 3 Tbsp olive oil
- 1 lemon, in wedges
- 8 green onions, white and green parts
- 4 thin slices of focaccia bread
- 1 clove garlic

Terrine of Sardines,

Heirloom Tomatoes, Zucchini and Basil

SERVES 6

Terrine

- 6 medium sardines (total weight 13 lbs), scaled, gutted and rinsed
- 2 Tbsp salt
- 2 cups water
- ½ cup olive oil + 4 Tbsp for brushing the fish and the zucchini
- 1 tsp fennel pollen
- 2 medium, firm zucchini, cut lengthwise into ⅛-inch slices
- 3 large heirloom tomatoes
- 4 slices white bread, crusts removed, soaked in 1 cup water
- 4 Tbsp tarama (salted cod roe)
- 1 small clove garlic, finely chopped
- Juice of 1 lemon
- ½ cup canola oil
- 1 cup white wine
- 2 shallots, minced
- 5 leaves gelatin, softened in cold water
- 1 cup whipping cream
- 1 cup whipped cream
- 16 leaves basil, stems removed
- 7 oz baby arugula
- Sprigs of fennel, for garnish

Fennel vinaigrette

- 1 bulb fennel
- Juice of ½ lemon
- ¼ cup good-quality olive oil

Tarama, a salted cod roe that is available from Greek grocery stores, adds flavour and helps to bind the layers of the terrine. If you cannot find fennel pollen, substitute ground fennel seeds.

Terrine On each sardine, make an incision behind both sides of the head to expose the spine. Place the sardine on its back, then pull the head slowly upwards and towards the tail. You should be able to pull out the spine with most of the tiny bones attached, although you will likely never get them all. Cut out the fins and the tail. Discard the heads, spines and fins.

In a medium bowl, dissolve the salt in the water. Add sardine fillets and let them sit in this brine for 10 minutes.

Preheat the oven to 350°F and line a baking sheet with parchment paper. Brush the sardines with olive oil and sprinkle lightly with fennel pollen. Place them on the baking sheet and bake for 2 to 3 minutes. Lifting the parchment paper, transfer the sardines to a cold baking sheet and refrigerate them for at least 10 minutes.

Preheat a grill to high. Brush zucchini slices with olive oil and grill on each side for 2 to 3 minutes, or until light grill marks are visible. Season with salt and pepper and allow to dry on a paper towel.

Fill a bowl with ice water. Bring a medium pot of water to a boil. Add tomatoes and blanch for 10 seconds, then plunge them into the ice bath. Peel the tomatoes, then quarter them and remove the seeds. Dry the tomatoes on several layers of paper towel.

Press out the moisture from the soaked bread and place the bread in a blender or food processor. Add tarama, garlic and lemon juice and purée. With the motor running, slowly add the ½ cup of olive oil and the canola oil.

In a small saucepan, heat wine and shallots on medium heat until liquid has reduced by half, about 5 minutes. Strain the wine reduction through a fine-mesh sieve into a bowl. Press out any excess moisture from the gelatin leaves and dissolve them in the warm reduction. Whisk this mixture into the tarama purée until well blended, then stir in whipping cream. Gently fold in whipped cream.

Lightly oil the inside of a 4-inch-deep terrine mould. Line the mould with plastic wrap, leaving 4 inches of plastic overhanging on each side. Spoon a ½-inch layer of the tarama mousse into the bottom of the terrine, then top it with 4 tomato quarters, side by side. Cover with a thin layer of mousse, place 4 basil leaves on top and press them gently into the mousse so that they are submerged. Layer grilled zucchini slices on top and cover with another thin layer of mousse. Top with 2 butterflied sardines, tail ends at the centre of the terrine, then cover with another layer of mousse. Continue layering tomatoes, basil, zucchini and sardines, with intervening thin layers of mousse, until you have used them all up. Finish with a ½-inch layer of mousse. Fold the overhanging plastic wrap over the top layer of mousse and refrigerate the terrine for 24 hours.

Fennel vinaigrette Extract the fennel juices in a juicer. (If you do not have a juicer, purée the fennel in a food processor with ½ cup of water and strain the juices through a cheesecloth.) Mix in lemon juice and your best olive oil until well emulsified, then season with salt and pepper.

To serve Unmould the terrine onto a cutting board, leaving the plastic wrap attached for easier handling. With an electric knife, cut three-quarter-inch slices and place one slice in the centre of six plates. Discard the plastic wrap. Surround the terrine slice with a quarter of the fennel vinaigrette and serve with baby arugula and sprigs of fennel.

Suggested wine A dry, medium-bodied white that shows spice, such as aligoté from Burgundy.

Sardine Escabeche

with Watercress, Grapefruit, Pink Peppercorns and Sake

SERVES 4 *as an entrée or 6 as an appetizer*

Sardine escabeche

- 12 small sardines (or 8 large ones), cleaned, scaled and heads removed
- 3/4 cup + 2 Tbsp olive oil
- 1 onion, thinly sliced
- 4 cloves garlic, thinly sliced
- 1 bulb fennel, thinly sliced
- 1 carrot, thinly sliced
- 2 sprigs thyme
- 2 bay leaves
- 1 Tbsp coriander seeds
- Zest of 1 orange
- Pinch of hot red chili flakes
- 1/2 cup red wine vinegar
- Juice of 2 lemons
- Pinch of fleur de sel, for garnish

Grapefruit salad

- 2 pink grapefruits
- 1 red onion, very thinly sliced
- 1 Tbsp pink peppercorns, crushed
- 1 bunch watercress, large stems removed

Citrus dressing

- 1/2 cup sake, boiled then chilled
- 1/2 cup grapefruit juice
- 1/4 cup olive oil
- 1/4 cup yuzu juice or lemon juice

Sardine escabeche Season sardines with salt. Heat 2 Tbsp of the olive oil in a large sauté pan on medium heat. Add sardines and brown on both sides, 1 to 2 minutes per side. Remove from the heat and arrange the sardines tightly in a deep baking dish and set aside.

In a saucepan, combine onion, garlic, fennel, carrot, thyme, bay leaves, coriander seeds, orange zest, chili flakes, vinegar and 6 Tbsp of the olive oil. Bring this mixture to a boil on high heat, then reduce the heat to medium and simmer for 10 minutes. Strain the liquid over the sardines while it is still hot. Then add the remaining 6 Tbsp of olive oil and the lemon juice. Cover the dish and refrigerate overnight.

Grapefruit salad Using a sharp knife, cut the peel off the grapefruits. Cut out the grapefruit segments between the membranes and place them in a large bowl. Discard the peel and the membranes. Add red onion, peppercorns and watercress and toss to combine.

Citrus dressing In a small bowl, whisk together all ingredients.

To serve Add the citrus dressing to the salad and toss to coat. Divide the salad among four or six plates. Arrange two to three sardines (without the marinade) on each plate and garnish with a pinch of fleur de sel.

Suggested wine Try a Sancerre from the Loire Valley that shows stone fruit and minerality.

Grilled Herring

with Fingerling Potatoes, Savoy Cabbage, Bacon and Caraway

SERVES 4

- 12 small fingerling potatoes
- 1/3 cup unsalted butter
- 2 slices of bacon, in thin strips
- 1 onion, thinly sliced
- 1 clove garlic, finely chopped
- 1 tsp caraway seeds
- 1 head Savoy cabbage, cored and thinly sliced
- 1/2 cup white wine
- 1 cup chicken stock (page 184)
- 3 to 4 sprigs parsley, chopped (about 1 Tbsp)
- 1 Tbsp Dijon mustard
- 1/2 lemon
- 8 fresh herrings, scaled, gutted and rinsed
- 1 Tbsp canola oil

Add potatoes to a medium pot of salted water. Bring to a boil and cook for about 10 minutes until potatoes are cooked through. Remove them from the water, allow to cool slightly and peel them.

Heat half of the butter in a large sauté pan on medium heat. Add bacon and render for 2 minutes, then add onion, garlic and caraway seeds and cook until fragrant, about 1 minute. Add Savoy cabbage, season with salt and pepper, and cook for 5 minutes, stirring frequently. Add wine and cook until wine has reduced completely, 3 to 4 minutes. Add chicken stock and cook for about 5 minutes until cabbage is done. Add parsley and potatoes, and heat until warmed through.

Drain the cabbage, straining the cooking liquid through a fine-mesh sieve into a saucepan. Reserve the cabbage and the potatoes. Whisk Dijon mustard and the remaining half of the butter into the liquid, then finish with a squeeze of lemon juice.

Preheat a grill to high. Brush herrings lightly with canola oil, season with salt and pepper and grill for 2 to 3 minutes on each side.

To serve On each of four plates, arrange two herrings. Heap a quarter of the cabbage and potatoes to the side and drizzle the dish with the mustard sauce.

Suggested wine Try a Champagne with some roundness and firm acidity. A blanc de blancs would work nicely.

Cured Herring Fillet

with Granny Smith Apple, Red Onions and Coriander

SERVES 4

Since the herrings will not be cooked, freeze them overnight before brining them in order to kill any potentially harmful parasites. Look for tempura flour at Japanese food stores.

Herring fillet In a medium saucepan, combine water, salt and sugar and bring to a boil on high heat. Remove from the heat, allow to cool, then chill this brine in the refrigerator.

On each herring, make an incision behind either side of the head to expose the spine. Place the herring on its back, then pull the head slowly upwards and towards the tail. This way you should be able to pull out most of the tiny bones, although you will likely never get them all. Cut out the fins, then cut the fillets off the bones and debone the flesh as much as possible. Discard heads, spines and fins. Place fillets in the cold brine for 1 hour, then lay them out on a dry towel and scrape off most of the skin. Cut the herring fillets into ¼-inch dice. Reserve a few pieces for garnish.

Peel and core one apple and cut it into ¼-inch dice. Core the remaining apple, then julienne on a mandolin.

In a small bowl, mix together sour cream, yogurt, mayonnaise, lemon juice, dill and chives. Season with salt and pepper. Add coriander seeds, red onion, diced apple and herrings.

Toss julienned apple with watercress, walnut oil and vinegar.

Onion beignets In a deep fryer or a deep pot, heat canola oil to 350°F.

In a small bowl, combine flour and water until just mixed. There will still be small lumps in the batter. Dip onion rings in the batter, then fry them for 1 minute or until golden brown. Remove from the oil and allow them to drain on several layers of paper towel. Season with salt.

To serve On each of four plates, arrange a quarter of the herring fillet in a line. Top with the reserved herring pieces and the apple salad. Arrange watercress around the plate and serve with a slice of pumpernickel bread and two onion beignets.

Suggested wine Stronger-flavoured fish fare well with sharp acidic wines. Try a Marlborough riesling.

Herring fillet

- 2 cups water
- ¼ cup salt
- 1 Tbsp sugar
- 4 frozen herrings, thawed and scaled
- 2 Granny Smith apples
- 2 Tbsp sour cream
- 1 Tbsp yogurt
- 1 Tbsp mayonnaise
- Juice of 1 lemon
- 1 Tbsp chopped dill
- 1 Tbsp chopped chives
- 1 Tbsp coriander seeds, toasted and crushed
- 2 Tbsp finely diced red onion
- 1 bunch baby watercress + a few sprigs for garnish
- 2 Tbsp walnut oil
- Dash of sherry vinegar
- 4 slices pumpernickel bread

Onion beignets

- 4 cups canola oil, for deep-frying
- ¼ cup tempura flour
- ¼ cup water, ice cold
- ½ small onion, cut in 8 thin rings

Green Sea Urchin

on a Buttered Baguette

SERVES 4

- 12 green sea urchins
- 12 slices of baguette
- 1 Tbsp unsalted butter, softened to room temperature
- 1 lemon, in 4 wedges

The most rewarding way to eat live sea urchin is the simplest—right out of the shell on lightly toasted and buttered slices of baguette. The edible part of the urchin is the roe found in the gonads, which are in five sections, are orange and have the texture of custard.

With sharp, pointy scissors, cut out a circle around the hole in each sea urchin. This is its mouth. Carefully remove the roe with a teaspoon and clean it in a bowl of cold salted water. Remove it from the water, dry on a kitchen towel, then transfer the roe to a small serving bowl. Discard the shells.

Preheat the broiler. Place the bread slices on a baking sheet. Broil until lightly toasted, then butter the bread and top with the roe.

To serve Place three slices of baguette on each plate. Finish with a squeeze of fresh lemon and freshly ground black pepper.

Suggested wine Try a well-balanced white with a fruity aroma and flavour, like the cortese varietal from Gavi Piedmont.

Green Sea Urchin

and Pacific Scallop Ceviche

SERVES 4

- 8 green sea urchins
- 8 medium fresh Pacific scallops, in eighths
- 2 Tbsp soy sauce
- 2 Tbsp yuzu juice
- Juice of 2 limes
- Pinch of freshly chopped garlic
- 1 tsp grated fresh ginger
- Pinch of seeded and minced hot red chili pepper
- 1 oz fresh wakame seaweed, rinsed and roughly chopped + extra for garnish
- 2 Tbsp thinly sliced red onion
- 2 to 3 red radishes, thinly sliced on a mandolin
- Handful of fresh cilantro leaves, chiffonaded (about 1/4 cup)
- 2 limes, sliced, for garnish

With sharp, pointy scissors, cut out a circle around the hole in each sea urchin. This is its mouth. Carefully remove the roe with a teaspoon and clean it in a bowl of cold salted water. Remove it from the water and dry on a kitchen towel. Wash the inside of the shells under cold water with a small brush. Turn them upside down on a kitchen towel to dry.

In a small bowl, combine scallops with soy sauce, yuzu juice, lime juice, garlic, ginger, chili pepper and salt to taste. Allow to marinate for 5 minutes, then add wakame, red onion, radishes and cilantro. Carefully fold in the sea urchin roe and mix well to combine.

To serve Divide the ceviche among the sea urchin shells. Serve two shells per person—arrange them on a platter of crushed ice decorated with lime slices and fresh seaweed.

Suggested wine This dish would be well complemented by something fresh, fruity and lively. Try a trebbiano, also known as ugni blanc.

Red Sea Urchin Roe

with White Asparagus and Blood Orange Sabayon

SERVES 4

- 1 tsp sugar
- 12 extra-large spears white asparagus, peeled
- 3 blood oranges
- 1 Tbsp lemon juice
- 3 organic egg yolks
- 1/4 cup sparkling white wine
- 3 Tbsp extra-virgin olive oil
- Pinch of espelette pepper + extra for garnish
- Pinch of chopped tarragon
- Roe from 4 large red sea urchins
- 2 sprigs chervil, stems removed, for garnish

Add sugar to a small pot of salted water and bring to a boil on high heat. Add asparagus and cook for 9 minutes. Remove the asparagus from the water and set aside on a warm plate.

With a sharp knife, cut the peel off 2 of the blood oranges. Cut out the segments between the membranes, working over a small saucepan to catch all the juices. Place the segments on a kitchen towel to dry. Juice the remaining orange into the saucepan, then heat the juice on medium heat until it has reduced to 1 Tbsp, 2 to 3 minutes. Discard the peels and membranes. Allow the reduction to cool, then add lemon juice.

In a small saucepan with sloping sides, whisk together egg yolks and sparkling wine over medium heat until the mixture becomes frothy and thickens to the point where you can draw lines on its surface. Remove the saucepan from the heat and slowly stir in olive oil until the mixture is emulsified. Add the blood orange–lemon reduction to this sabayon and season with salt and espelette pepper. Finish the sabayon with tarragon.

To serve Cut asparagus in half on a gentle bias and place three bottom halves slightly off centre on each of four warm plates. Spoon a quarter of the sabayon over the asparagus. Lean three asparagus tips on the asparagus bottoms at a 45-degree angle. Arrange the roe from one sea urchin over the asparagus and garnish with a quarter of the blood orange segments and chervil sprigs. Finish with a sprinkle of espelette pepper.

Suggested wine A white Bordeaux, such as a blend of sauvignon blanc and sémillon.

Red Sea Urchin

in a Cucumber Vichyssoise with Kusshi Oysters and Lemon Cream

SERVES 4

Vichyssoise is a creamy French-style soup made with puréed leeks, onions and potatoes and traditionally served cold. Red sea urchins are larger than the smaller and sweeter green urchins. Preparing the urchins for this dish can be a bit messy—don an apron and work over a baking sheet with a generous lip to catch all of the juices that run out.

Vichyssoise In a medium pot, melt butter over medium-high heat and sweat leeks and onion with a good pinch of salt and several turns of pepper for about 5 minutes until tender but not browned. Add potatoes and chicken stock and simmer for 35 minutes until potatoes are tender.

Add cream, then transfer this soup to a food processor and purée while gradually adding the raw cucumber slices.

Strain the purée through a medium-mesh sieve into a clean bowl. Season to taste, then refrigerate until chilled, about 1 hour.

Lemon cream In a small bowl, combine cream, lemon zest, tarragon, lemon juice, cayenne and a pinch of salt.

Sea urchin and oysters Place a small cutting board in the centre of a baking sheet. Place each sea urchin, mouth-side up, on the cutting board and crack it open with a heavy chef's knife without smashing completely through the urchin. Alternatively, with sharp, pointy scissors, cut a 1-inch circle around the hole in each sea urchin. This is its mouth. Empty the liquid inside the shell onto the baking sheet, then strain it into a small bowl. With a teaspoon, carefully remove the roe from each sea urchin and wash in a bowl of cold salted water to remove any grit. Discard the shells.

To serve Ladle three-quarters of a cup of the vichyssoise into four soup bowls, then garnish with the sea urchin roe and the oysters. Scoop a spoonful of lemon cream into the centre of each bowl and sprinkle with chives and cucumber.

Suggested wine Complement the creaminess of this dish with a Roero Arneis from Piedmont.

Vichyssoise

- 3 Tbsp unsalted butter
- 12 oz leeks, white part only, thinly sliced
- 1/2 small onion, thinly sliced
- 4 oz potatoes, thinly sliced
- 1 2/3 cups chicken stock (page 184)
- 3/4 cup table cream (18% milk fat)
- 1 English cucumber, peeled, seeded and sliced

Lemon cream

- 1 cup whipped cream
- Zest of 1/2 lemon
- 1 tsp chopped tarragon leaves
- 1 tsp lemon juice
- Pinch of cayenne

Sea urchin and oysters

- 4 medium red sea urchins
- 12 kusshi oysters, shucked
- 1 Tbsp minced chives, for garnish
- 1 Tbsp finely diced cucumber, for garnish
- 4 to 8 sprigs watercress, for garnish

Humboldt Squid "Pasta"

with Fennel and Sea Urchin Sauce

SERVES 4

- Roe from 4 sea urchins, cleaned
- 1 cup white wine sauce (page 188)
- 1 tsp lemon juice + extra for garnish
- Pinch of espelette pepper + extra for garnish
- 1 lb large Humboldt squid tubes, cleaned and thinly sliced lengthwise on a mandolin
- 1 Tbsp olive oil
- 1 large bulb fennel, halved, cored and thinly sliced on a mandolin and greens reserved for garnish
- 1 onion, halved and thinly sliced
- 1 clove garlic, thinly sliced on a mandolin
- 1 Tbsp chiffonaded Italian parsley leaves

This dish is an example of how squid, if properly cooked, can have the look and pleasant al dente feel of noodles.

In a small saucepan, cook half of the sea urchin roe in white wine sauce on low heat for 2 minutes. Mix in a blender and season with lemon juice, salt and espelette pepper.

Fill a large bowl with ice water. Bring a large pot of salted water to a boil. Add the squid "pasta" and blanch for 5 seconds. Drain the squid, then plunge it into the ice bath to refresh it.

In a medium sauté pan, heat olive oil on medium heat. Add fennel, onion and garlic and sweat until fragrant and just cooked, 3 to 4 minutes. Add squid pasta, parsley and the remaining half of the sea urchin roe to the fennel. Add warm sea urchin sauce and toss to coat.

To serve Divide the squid pasta, fennel and sauce among four small soup bowls. Season with espelette pepper and a squeeze of fresh lemon juice and garnish with the fennel greens.

Suggested wine Try a viognier with some sweetness—look for a French Vin de Pays D'Oc.

Humboldt Squid

Braised in Tomato-Oregano Sauce with Creamy Polenta

SERVES 4

Squid

1 small Humboldt squid, about 5 lbs
4 Tbsp olive oil + extra for garnish
1 onion, finely diced
2 ribs celery, finely diced
1 carrot, finely diced
6 cloves garlic, finely chopped
Pinch of hot red chili flakes
1 Tbsp dried oregano
2 cups crushed tomatoes
1 cup water
1/4 cup Italian parsley, chopped
1/4 cup basil leaves, chopped

Polenta

2 cups chicken stock (page 184)
2 cups milk (2% or homogenized)
1 tsp salt
1/4 cup olive oil
1 cup finely ground cornmeal
1/2 cup table cream (18% milk fat)
5 Tbsp unsalted butter
4 oz grated Parmesan

Squid Remove the head from the squid and cut out the beak and the eyes. With a sharp knife, peel the body and remove the cartilage from the inside of the squid. Wash the head and tentacles thoroughly under running water. Cut the tentacles into 1-inch pieces and the tube into 1-inch squares.

In a large sauté pan, heat olive oil on medium heat. Add onion, celery, carrot, garlic, chili flakes and oregano until the vegetables are fragrant and soft, 5 to 10 minutes. Add squid pieces and cook for 5 minutes. Add crushed tomatoes and water and simmer at low temperature for 1½ to 2 hours until squid becomes very tender and the mix resembles a thick ragout.

Polenta In a large pot, bring chicken stock and milk to a simmer, then add the salt and olive oil. While stirring constantly with a wooden spoon, slowly pour in the cornmeal. Cook on low heat for 30 to 40 minutes, stirring frequently, until polenta is smooth and soft. Add cream, butter and Parmesan. Season with freshly ground black pepper. If the polenta is too thick, add a little water.

To serve Finish the squid ragout with parsley and basil and a drizzle of extra-virgin olive oil. Divide the polenta among four bowls. Ladle a quarter of the squid and tomato-oregano sauce over each serving.

Suggested wine Pair this dish with a youthful red wine that is crisp and fruity—try a Bardolino Superiore from Veneto.

Octopus Ceviche

with Rocoto Pepper Sauce

SERVES 4

Flavouring this ceviche is a sauce made with the rocoto chili—a round, red Peruvian chili pepper. If you cannot find it, substitute a red jalapeño. The octopus in this dish is cooked in salted water until very tender. Some chefs suggest that adding cork to the water will make the octopus more tender, but at Blue Water Cafe we have not noticed cork making any difference—instead, we find that tenderness is a result of the cooking time. Serve this dish with corn nuts, wasabi peas or fried chickpeas (page 96).

Ceviche Bring a large pot of salted water to a boil on high heat. Add octopus and boil for 1 to 1½ hours, until the tentacles just about come away from the head when you try to pull the octopus out of the water with a pair of tongs. Slice 4 of the octopus tentacles into ¼-inch pieces. Reserve the rest of the octopus for another recipe.

In a large bowl, combine sliced octopus, celery, red onion, sweet potatoes, garlic, cilantro and lime juice. Season well with salt and allow the mixture to marinate for 5 minutes.

Chili sauce Combine celery, leek, onion, garlic, bell peppers and rocoto pepper in a medium pot and add just enough water to cover. Bring to a boil on high heat and cook for 10 minutes until vegetables are tender. Drain, allow to cool slightly, then purée this mixture in a blender or food processor. Strain through a fine-mesh sieve into a bowl, then refrigerate for at least 30 minutes. When ready to serve, stir in mayonnaise and lime juice.

To serve Spoon two tablespoons of the rocoto chili sauce into each of four martini glasses and top it with a quarter of the ceviche.

Suggested wine Try a dry and crisp riesling from the Clare Valley.

Ceviche

- 1 octopus, about 4 lbs, cleaned
- 2 ribs celery, thinly sliced
- ¼ red onion, thinly sliced
- ¼ cup diced cooked sweet potatoes
- 1 clove garlic, finely chopped
- 2 Tbsp chopped cilantro
- Juice of 2 limes

Chili sauce

- 1 rib celery, chopped
- 1 small leek, white part only, chopped
- ¼ onion, chopped
- 1 clove garlic, chopped
- 2 red bell peppers, seeded and chopped
- 1 rocoto pepper, seeded and chopped
- ¼ cup mayonnaise
- Juice of 2 limes

Grilled Octopus

with Carrot-Anchovy Salad and Parsley Sauce

SERVES 4

For a more dramatic presentation, leave the octopus tentacles whole rather than cutting them into pieces. At the restaurant, we use the suction cups as a garnish.

Octopus Combine octopus, onion, garlic, celery, carrot, thyme, bay leaves, water and salt in a large stockpot and bring to a boil on high heat. Reduce the heat to medium-low and simmer for 1½ hours, or until an octopus tentacle separates easily from the body. Remove from the heat and allow the octopus to cool in the liquid.

Remove the octopus from the cooking broth, transfer to a large bowl and refrigerate for 1 hour. Cut octopus into 2-inch pieces, skin and suction cups still attached.

Preheat a grill to high. Season the octopus with salt and black pepper and toss in 4 Tbsp of olive oil, then place on the hot grill until char marks appear (the skin might come off in some places), about 5 minutes. Remove the octopus immediately to avoid drying out the centre and transfer to a bowl. Add vinegar and the remaining 6 Tbsp of olive oil and toss until well coated.

Carrot-anchovy salad Combine all ingredients in a medium bowl and mix well. Season with salt and pepper and set aside.

Parsley sauce Combine parsley, green onions, lemon zest, garlic, olive oil and a pinch of salt in a blender and purée until smooth. Stir in capers and season with a squeeze of lemon juice.

To serve On each of four plates, heap a quarter of the carrot-anchovy salad. Place a quarter of the grilled octopus beside the salad and drizzle the octopus with the parsley sauce.

Suggested wine A more complex sparkling wine with medium body, like a Californian blanc de noirs.

Octopus

- 4 lbs octopus, cleaned
- 1 onion, quartered
- 1 bulb garlic, halved
- 1 rib celery
- 1 large carrot
- 1 bunch fresh thyme
- 2 bay leaves
- 20 cups cold water
- 3 Tbsp salt
- ½ cup + 2 Tbsp extra-virgin olive oil
- 3 Tbsp sherry vinegar

Carrot-anchovy salad

- 2 large carrots, julienned into 2-inch strips on a mandolin
- ¼ cup Italian parsley leaves, chiffonaded
- 2 anchovy fillets, finely diced
- 1 small clove garlic, germ removed, finely chopped
- Juice of ½ lemon
- Pinch of sugar

Parsley sauce

- 1 bunch Italian parsley
- 1 bunch green onions, green part only
- Zest of 1 lemon
- 2 cloves garlic, germ removed
- ½ cup olive oil
- 2 Tbsp capers, rinsed and finely chopped
- ½ lemon

Octopus Confit

with Chickpeas and Roasted Red Peppers

SERVES 4

Octopus confit

- 1 bulb garlic, halved through the equator
- 1 onion, quartered
- 1 red jalapeño pepper
- 1 small bunch fresh thyme
- 1 sprig dried oregano
- 1 Tbsp fennel seeds
- 2 bay leaves
- 2 lbs octopus, thoroughly washed and rinsed
- 4 cups olive oil

Chickpeas and peppers

- 4 red bell peppers
- 7 Tbsp olive oil
- 1/2 cup oil from the octopus confit
- 2 shallots, thinly sliced
- 9 cloves garlic, 6 thinly sliced on a mandolin and 3 cut in half
- 7 oz cooked chickpeas (about 1 cup)
- 12 slices baguette, each 1/4 inch thick
- Juice of 1 lemon
- Dash of red wine vinegar
- 1/2 cup basil leaves, coarsely chopped
- 1/2 cup Italian parsley leaves, coarsely chopped

Octopus confit In a pot just large enough to hold the octopus snugly, combine garlic, onion, jalapeño, thyme, oregano, fennel seeds and bay leaves, then place the octopus on top and add olive oil until the octopus is covered. Cook on medium heat for about 1½ hours, or until a paring knife easily pierces the shoulder between the head and the tentacles.

Remove the pot from the heat and allow the octopus to cool in the oil. Once cool, remove the octopus from the oil and place it on a clean cutting board. Reserve the oil. Using a sharp knife, cut the tentacles—with skin and suction cups still attached—into bite-size pieces. Cut off and discard the octopus beak, then slice the remainder of the head into thin strips about 2 inches long. Set aside.

Chickpeas and peppers Preheat the oven to 400°F. Brush bell peppers with 1 Tbsp of olive oil and set them on a baking sheet. Roast for 15 to 20 minutes until the skins are lightly charred. Transfer to a metal bowl and cover with plastic wrap. Allow to cool for 30 minutes.

Peel the bell peppers, then cut them open and remove and discard the seeds. Cut the pepper flesh into wide strips about 2 inches long.

Heat the octopus confit oil in a medium pot on low heat. Add shallots and the thinly sliced garlic and sweat until fragrant, about 5 minutes. Add chickpeas and roasted peppers and cook for 10 minutes.

Heat 6 Tbsp of olive oil in a sauté pan on medium heat. Add baguette slices and pan-fry on both sides until golden brown and crunchy, about 2 minutes. Drain on paper towels to absorb the excess moisture, then rub croutons with garlic halves.

To serve In a large bowl, combine octopus pieces, chickpeas and roasted peppers. Add salt, lemon juice and vinegar, then mix in basil and parsley. Divide this mixture among four bowls. Top each bowl with a quarter of the croutons.

Suggested wine Go for something off the beaten path—Greco di Tufo shows lemon and clove with good fruit and a lively finish.

Whelk "Escargot Style"

in Parsley, Garlic and Seaweed Butter

SERVES 4

Rinse whelk meat in a bowl of cold water and dry with a kitchen towel. In a medium sauté pan, melt unsalted butter over medium heat until it starts to foam. Add garlic, green onion, nori and parsley and cook over low heat for 1 minute. Add whelk meat, white wine and brandy and cook over medium heat for 5 minutes until whelk is heated through. Season with salt and pepper. Finish with lemon juice.

To serve Place in small individual bowls with toasted country bread slices to soak up the butter.

Suggested wine Try Bret Brothers' Pouilly-Vinzelles, an elegant, full-bodied chardonnay with under-toned oak.

- 36 pieces cooked whelk meat
- ½ cup unsalted butter
- 1 clove garlic, finely chopped
- 4 green onions, thinly sliced
- 1 Tbsp nori seaweed powder
- 1 densely packed cup of Italian parsley leaves, finely chopped
- 1 oz white wine
- Dash of brandy
- 1 tsp lemon juice
- Toasted country bread slices

Whelk Risotto

with Basil, Garlic, Chili and Parmesan

SERVES 4

Risotto

- 2 cups chicken stock (page 184)
- 5 Tbsp olive oil
- ½ small onion, minced
- 1 sprig thyme
- ¾ cup vialone nano rice
- 4 Tbsp dry white wine
- 5 Tbsp unsalted butter
- ¼ cup freshly grated Parmesan

Whelk

- 24 pieces cooked whelk meat
- 7 Tbsp olive oil
- 2 slices French bread, each 2 inches thick, crusts removed, diced
- 2 shallots, minced
- 1 clove garlic, chopped
- Pinch of hot red chili flakes
- 2 Roma tomatoes, seeded and diced
- 3 Tbsp white wine
- 8 basil leaves, torn into small pieces
- ½ lemon

Vialone nano rice is a small starchy grain that makes a very creamy risotto. Look for it in Italian food stores.

Risotto In a medium saucepan, bring chicken stock to a gentle simmer on medium heat.

In a medium saucepan with sloping sides, heat olive oil over medium heat. Add onion and thyme and cook until the onions are fragrant and translucent, about 2 minutes.

Add rice and stir constantly with a wooden spoon for about 5 minutes, until the outside of the grains becomes somewhat glossy and the white starchy centre can be seen.

Deglaze the saucepan with wine and cook over medium-low heat until the wine has been absorbed, about 5 minutes. Add a quarter of the hot chicken stock to the rice and cook, stirring frequently, until the liquid has been absorbed. Continue adding the rest of the chicken stock, one ladleful at a time, waiting until each ladleful has been absorbed before adding the next, until the rice is cooked but still a little al dente. (You may not need all the chicken stock.) This process takes 15 to 18 minutes.

Once the stock has been fully absorbed, remove the thyme and add butter and Parmesan. Stir carefully with a wooden spoon so as not to break the cooked rice grains. Season with salt and pepper. The risotto should be creamy but not too runny.

Whelk In a small sauté pan, heat 4 Tbsp of olive oil on medium heat. Add bread and cook until golden, about 2 minutes.

In a medium sauté pan, heat 2 Tbsp of olive oil on high heat. Add whelk pieces and sauté briefly until lightly seared, about 30 seconds. Remove them from the pan and set them aside in a bowl. Add the remaining 1 Tbsp of olive oil to the pan and add shallots, garlic and chili flakes. Sauté until fragrant, about 1 minute.

Add tomatoes and stir for 1 minute, then deglaze the pan with wine and continue to cook until liquid has reduced by three-quarters, about 30 seconds.

Add cooked whelk, basil and croutons. Season with salt, pepper and a squeeze of lemon juice.

To serve Divide the risotto among four bowls. Top each bowl with a quarter of the whelk mixture.

Suggested wine Try a muscadet, which is crisp with citrus and minerally notes.

Periwinkles
with Aioli

SERVES 4

Periwinkles Combine all of the ingredients in a large pot and fill the pot with cold water. Bring the pot to a boil on high heat, then remove it from the heat. Allow the periwinkles to cool in the liquid.

Aioli In a small bowl, combine olive and canola oils.

In a medium bowl, whisk together egg yolks and garlic. Add mixed oils in a thin stream while continuing to whisk to obtain a creamy emulsion. Season with a squeeze of lemon juice and a pinch of salt.

To serve Divide the periwinkles evenly among four bowls and serve them with individual ramekins of aioli. Provide each guest with a toothpick to extract the periwinkles from their shells, removing the little black cap that covers the opening of each snail before eating.

Suggested wine A white wine with gentle acidity and typical honey. Try a chenin blanc from the Loire Valley.

Periwinkles

- 4½ lbs fresh periwinkles
- 3 shallots, sliced
- 1 rib celery, in ¼-inch slices
- 6 garlic cloves, crushed
- 4 sprigs thyme
- 2 bay leaves
- ½ cup white wine
- 2 Tbsp salt

Aioli

- ½ cup olive oil
- ½ cup canola oil
- 2 egg yolks
- 6 cloves garlic, germ removed, finely chopped
- ½ lemon

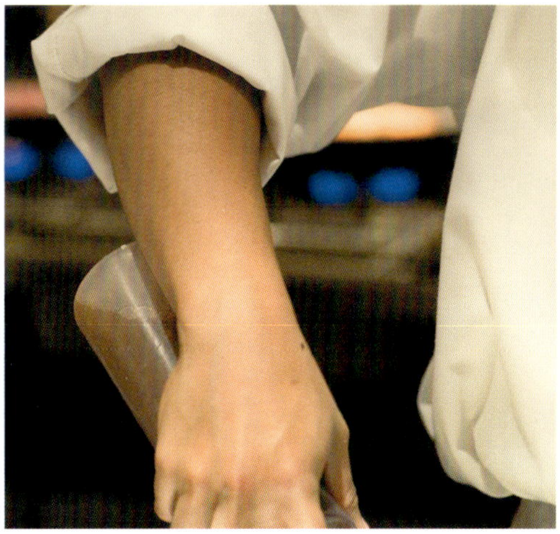

Periwinkles

with Stinging Nettle Purée and Potato Chips

SERVES 4

Periwinkles

- 4 Tbsp unsalted butter
- 1 bunch green onions, white parts only, thinly sliced
- 3 cloves garlic, thinly sliced on a mandolin
- 4½ lbs periwinkles, cooked as on page 149
- ½ cup chiffonaded Italian parsley leaves
- ½ lemon

Stinging nettle purée

- 1 lb stinging nettles, stems removed
- 5 Tbsp unsalted butter
- 1 bunch green onions, green parts only
- 1 clove garlic, finely chopped
- ⅓ cup cooking liquid from the periwinkles
- 2 Tbsp whipping cream

Potato chips

- 1 large russet potato, peeled and thinly sliced on a mandolin, then rinsed in very cold water for 30 minutes
- 4 cups canola oil, for deep-frying

Stinging nettles are rich in vitamins A, C and D and in the minerals iron, potassium, magnesium and calcium. Blanching the nettles removes their sting, but wear gloves when handling the uncooked plants. If stinging nettles are not available at your local specialty food store, use spinach instead.

Periwinkles In a large sauté pan, melt butter on medium heat. Add green onions and garlic and cook for 2 minutes. Once the mixture is fragrant, add cooked periwinkles and season with salt, pepper, parsley and a squeeze of lemon juice.

Stinging nettle purée Fill a large bowl with ice water. Bring a medium pot of salted water to a boil on high heat. Add stinging nettles and blanch for 2 minutes, then plunge them into the ice bath to refresh. Drain the stinging nettles and press out any excess moisture.

In a small sauté pan, heat butter on medium heat. Add green onions and garlic and sauté for 2 minutes. Add stinging nettles, cooking liquid from the periwinkles and cream. Bring this mixture to a boil, then remove the pan from the heat, allow the mixture to cool slightly, then purée the mixture in a blender. Season with salt.

Potato chips Drain the potato slices and dry them well on kitchen towels.

Heat canola oil in a deep fryer or a deep pot to 350°F (use a thermometer to check the temperature). Add potato slices and cook until light golden and crisp, 30 to 60 seconds. Remove the chips from the oil and allow them to drain on paper towels. Season with salt and coarsely ground black pepper.

To serve Divide the stinging nettle purée evenly among four bowls. Top with the periwinkles and serve with the potato chips on the side.

Suggested wine Try a chenin blanc from South Africa with some spice and greenness.

Poached Gooseneck Barnacles

SERVES 4

Gooseneck barnacles have a strong but pleasing taste that is both salty and slightly sweet. They are now being farmed, so they can be found in some specialty fish markets.

- 48 to 72 gooseneck barnacles
- 8 cups vegetable stock (page 184)
- 3 to 5 cloves garlic, thinly sliced
- ½ lb unsalted butter (about 1 cup)
- 12 wedges of fresh lemon

Thoroughly rinse barnacles, rubbing them gently to dislodge any sand.

In a large pot, combine vegetable stock and barnacles. Bring this mixture to a boil on high heat, reduce the heat to medium and cook for 2 minutes until the base of the barnacles turns a deep pink. Remove the barnacles and divide them among 4 bowls.

In a small saucepan, combine garlic and butter and heat on medium heat for 1 minute, until the butter has melted and infused with the garlic.

To serve Serve the barnacles with individual ramekins of garlic butter and wedges of lemon. Have each guest peel off the outer skin of the barnacle using the shell as a handle—the inside is the edible part—and season the pinkish neck meat with lemon juice and drawn garlic butter. Offer guests small bowls of warm lemon water to clean their fingers and napkins to protect their clothing, since barnacles sometimes secrete an orange-coloured dye when they are eaten.

Suggested wine A lighter-style wine with a crisp character—try a pinot grigio from Veneto.

Gooseneck Barnacles Provençale

SERVES 4

- 48 to 72 gooseneck barnacles
- 3 Roma tomatoes
- ½ cup + 2 Tbsp olive oil
- 2 shallots, minced
- 3 cloves garlic, thinly sliced
- 1 Tbsp chopped fresh tarragon
- Pinch of espelette pepper
- Dash of Pernod
- 1 cup dry white wine
- ½ lemon
- 16 slices baguette
- ½ cup aioli (page 149)

Thoroughly rinse barnacles under cold water, rubbing them gently to dislodge any sand.

Fill a medium bowl with ice water. Bring a medium pot of water to a boil on high heat. Add tomatoes and blanch for 30 seconds. Remove from the water and plunge them into the ice bath. Peel and seed the tomatoes, then dice the tomato flesh.

Heat 4 Tbsp of the olive oil in a large pot. Add shallots and garlic and cook on medium heat for 1 minute until fragrant. Add tomatoes, tarragon, espelette pepper and a pinch of salt. Cook for 1 minute. Add barnacles, cook for 1 minute, then add Pernod and wine. Cover the pot with a lid and steam for 4 minutes. Finish with a squeeze of lemon juice.

Heat 6 Tbsp of olive oil in a sauté pan on medium heat. Add baguette slices and pan-fry on both sides until golden brown and crunchy, about 2 minutes. Drain on paper towels to absorb the excess moisture.

To serve Divide the barnacles evenly among four bowls and serve with the croutons and a bowl of aioli on the side.

Suggested wine A number of unoaked chardonnays would work here—try one from western Australia or the Okanagan Valley.

Jellyfish and Asian Pear Salad

SERVES 4

Jellyfish salad Rinse jellyfish under cold water and drain. Cover with boiling water and allow it to stand for 10 minutes, then drain and rinse again under a slow stream of cold running water for 30 minutes. Drain the jellyfish and pat dry with a kitchen towel.

In a bowl, mix together olive oil and lemon juice to make a marinade. Season with salt and black pepper. Combine the jellyfish and the marinade in a resealable zip-top bag and allow to refrigerate overnight.

In a large bowl, toss together jellyfish, peas, bean sprouts, carrots, Asian pear, mixed herbs and green onions.

Red pepper broth In a small bowl, dissolve the palm sugar in the fish sauce.

In a food processor, combine bell peppers, jalapeños, ginger, garlic, lemon grass, cilantro, the sugar–fish sauce mixture and one ice cube and blend until the mixture is puréed. Add lime juice and blend again to mix. Strain this mixture through a fine-mesh sieve and season with salt.

To serve Toss the salad with a quarter of the red pepper broth. Divide the salad among four bowls, and pour the remaining broth overtop.

Suggested wine A Spanish verdejo tends to show pear and honey flavours with some nuttiness, which would match this salad perfectly.

Jellyfish salad

- 9 oz dried shredded jellyfish
- 1/4 cup olive oil
- 1 Tbsp lemon juice
- 10 snap peas, strings removed, julienned lengthwise
- 1 oz bean sprouts
- 2 small carrots, peeled and thinly sliced on a mandolin
- 1/2 Asian pear, peeled, cored and julienned on a mandolin
- 1/2 cup mixed herbs, such as fresh cilantro, spicy globe basil and Italian parsley leaves
- 2 green onions, thinly sliced

Red pepper broth

- 1 1/2 Tbsp palm sugar
- 2 Tbsp fish sauce
- 2 red bell peppers, seeded and roughly chopped
- 2 red jalapeño peppers, seeded and roughly chopped
- 1-inch piece of ginger, roughly chopped
- 1 clove garlic, roughly chopped
- 4-inch segment of lemon grass stem, roughly chopped
- 4 sprigs cilantro
- 5 Tbsp fresh lime juice

Sesame-marinated Jellyfish
with Cucumber and Daikon

SERVES 4

Jellyfish is great flavour carrier with a crunchy texture. Dried jellyfish can be found in specialty Asian markets.

Rinse jellyfish under cold water and drain. Cover with boiling water and allow it to stand for 10 minutes, then drain and rinse again under a slow stream of cold running water for 30 minutes. Drain the jellyfish and pat it dry with a kitchen towel.

In bowl, mix together sesame oil, vinegar, sugar, soy sauce, togarashi and toasted sesame seeds to make a marinade. Combine the jellyfish and the marinade in a resealable zip-top bag and allow to refrigerate overnight.

Meanwhile, rinse daikon under cold water for 10 minutes.

To serve Line the inside of four wide-mouth or martini glasses with the cucumber slices. Cover with a layer of daikon and top with marinated jellyfish. Garnish with black sesame seeds and a pinch of togarashi.

Suggested wine This dish would come alive with a refreshing bubble, such as that of Prosecco di Conegliano from Veneto.

- 9 oz dried shredded jellyfish
- 1/4 cup sesame oil
- 2 tsp unseasoned rice vinegar
- 2 tsp sugar
- 2 tsp soy sauce
- 1 tsp shichimi togarashi (Japanese seven-spice seasoning) + pinch for garnish
- 1 Tbsp sesame seeds, toasted
- 4-inch piece of daikon radish, peeled and julienned (about 1 cup)
- 1 English cucumber, thinly sliced
- 1 Tbsp black sesame seeds

Mixed Seaweed Salad

with Avocado and Japanese Cucumber

SERVES 4

1/3 cup extra-virgin olive oil
1 Tbsp soy sauce
2 Tbsp lemon juice
2 green onions, thinly sliced
2 ripe avocados, peeled and stone removed
2 oz mixed dehydrated seaweed, reconstituted in cold water
1 Japanese cucumber, sliced on a mandolin

Packages of mixed seaweed are available commercially at Japanese food stores. They usually include several varieties, including kombu, wakame and hijiki. Japanese cucumber is similar to English cucumber but has a bumpier skin.

In a small bowl, make a dressing by whisking together olive oil, soy sauce and lemon juice. Add green onions.

To serve Cut each avocado half into thin slices, then fan the slices of each half out onto a plate. Spoon one teaspoon of dressing over each of the avocado halves and sprinkle with coarse sea salt. In a medium bowl, toss seaweed and cucumber with the rest of the dressing and divide this salad among the four plates, placing it on top of the avocado.

Suggested wine Sake works well with seaweed. Try a junmai ginjo sake.

Wakame Seaweed Salad

with Asian Pear, Ginger and Sesame

SERVES 4 · SHOWN AT RIGHT

1/4 cup rice wine vinegar
1/4 cup soy sauce
1/4 cup sesame oil
Dash of ponzu juice
1 tsp freshly grated ginger
2 green onions, thinly sliced
2 oz of dehydrated wakame seaweed, reconstituted in water and cut into 2-inch strips
1 Asian pear, peeled, cored and thinly sliced
1 bunch watercress
1 Tbsp sesame seeds, toasted, for garnish

In a medium bowl, whisk together vinegar, soy sauce, sesame oil, ponzu, ginger and green onions. In a large bowl, combine wakame, Asian pear and watercress. Add dressing and toss to coat.

To serve Divide salad among four plates and garnish with sesame seeds.

Suggested wine This salad is a little sweeter, so you could pair it with a light pinot gris.

RAW BAR

RAW BAR

THE RAW BAR sits in its own serene space a few paces west of the main bar and south of the main dining room. It has a dozen seats—high chairs that surround the bar in a semi-circle. The lighting is judiciously different from the rest of the room, somehow more focussed on the bar top and the preparation counter, where Chef Masaaki Kudo and his assistant chefs ply their artful craft.

The Raw Bar is a destination unto itself for many diners at Blue Water Cafe, a pivotal starting point for the evening. But even if clients go straight to their table, they almost always begin with something from Masa's bar. He says his food is about technique, experience and presentation, but the core of everything Masa does is always the fish.

There are plenty of complementary creations at Blue Water Cafe. Frank Pabst and Masa consult daily and ensure clients are getting the best of both worlds: a classical, innovative sushi bar and a fine-dining room. Both chefs prepare certain fish in different ways, but Yoshi uses highly particular ingredients as well. They fuel his imagination, but they also fuel Blue Water Cafe's overarching philosophy: only the finest products, the finest preparations and the finest service.

Geoduck, a delicacy in Japanese cuisine for centuries, are now prized also on the Pacific Coast—and at Blue Water Cafe. These bivalves are clams, though their distinctive, trunk-like external appendage makes them unique. This appendage, a nutrient siphon for the animals, is their most flavourful component. Yoshi uses it to great advantage.

Hawaiian yellowtail (Kona Kampachi) are not to be confused with yellowfin tuna. The former belong to the jack family of fish and are close cousins of the Japanese yellowtail (hamachi). The hatch-to-harvest farming technique used by Kona Blue Water Farms in Hawaii is a sustainable and environmentally sound method for growing these healthy and great-tasting fish.

The Raw Bar is a microcosm, then, of Blue Water Cafe itself. Creativity, experience, dedication and the best of the ocean's provenance are combined to create a fine-dining experience like no other.

Albacore Tuna Mizore-ae

SERVES 1

- 4 oz albacore tuna loin, cleaned
- 2 oz daikon radish, finely grated
- 4 Tbsp ponzu shoyu (page 189)
- 6 Tbsp tosazu sauce (page 189)
- 3 shiso leaves, finely chopped

Lightly season the tuna with salt and allow it to sit for 5 to 6 minutes. Using a kitchen torch, sear the tuna for 2 minutes on each side and cut it into 5 or 6 even pieces.

Rinse the grated daikon with cold water, then quickly drain and squeeze out any excess moisture. The rinsing removes the daikon's strong odour.

In a small bowl, stir together ponzu shoyu and tosazu sauce. Add this mixture to the daikon and toss to coat.

To serve Place tuna pieces on a plate. Top with daikon and garnish with shiso leaves.

Suggested wine A junmai-level sake would offer the right amount of dryness with a creamy finish.

Albacore Tuna Goma-ae

SERVES 1

- 4½ oz albacore tuna loin, cleaned
- 2 Tbsp wasabi powder
- ½ cup soy sauce
- ¼ cup mirin
- 3 Tbsp sake
- 4 Tbsp ground sesame seeds
- 1 green onion, soaked in cold water for 10 minutes, then drained and thinly sliced

Ground sesame seeds are available at Asian supermarkets. They have the consistency of a powder rather than a paste like tahini.

Cut albacore tuna into 8 even cubes.

In a medium bowl, mix about 1 tsp of cold water into the wasabi powder until it reaches a firm consistency. Stir in soy sauce, mirin, sake and ground sesame seeds until well blended. Add tuna pieces and toss to coat.

To serve Extract the tuna pieces from the sauce and place them on a plate. Top with slices of green onion.

Suggested wine A dry wine with minerality and stone fruit, such as arneis from Piedmont, would be ideal.

Albacore Tuna Tartare

SERVES 1 · SHOWN AT LEFT

Toro, the fatty belly meat of the tuna, has a luxurious flavour and texture. Garnish with shredded dried red chili or thinly sliced deep-fried wonton skin.

Using a kitchen torch, sear the toro for 1 minute on each side and cut it into ¼-inch cubes. Toss it with red onion in a small bowl and lightly season with salt and chili flakes. In a separate bowl, sprinkle ahi tuna with salt.

Spoon a layer of the toro mixture into a 2-inch ring mould. Top with a layer of ahi tuna. Continue alternating layers until the fish has been used up. Press down on the tartare with the back of a spoon so that it keeps its shape.

In a small bowl, whisk about ½ tsp of water into the powdered mustard to get a thick paste. Mix in the tama miso, then use the vinegar to thin the mixture to the consistency of a cream sauce.

To serve Spoon two tablespoons of the sauce onto a plate and top with the tuna tartare. Remove the ring mould and serve.

Suggested wine Try a lighter sauvignon blanc from the Maipo Valley.

- 3 oz albacore tuna toro
- 1 tsp finely chopped red onion
- Pinch of Japanese chili flakes
- 1/2 oz ahi (bigeye) tuna loin, cleaned and cut in 1/4-inch cubes
- 1 tsp dry mustard powder
- 1 Tbsp tama miso (page 189)
- 1 tsp Japanese rice vinegar

Bigeye Tuna Tataki

SERVES 1

Shiro-negi is a Japanese leek also known as Welsh onion. It is available at Japanese and Chinese markets, or substitute the white part of a green onion. Moromi miso is a dark miso paste made with barley and can be found at Asian supermarkets.

Sprinkle tuna with salt and allow it to sit for 5 minutes. Using a kitchen torch, lightly sear the tuna for 5 minutes, or until lightly browned on all sides. Refrigerate the tuna until it is cool.

In a medium bowl, whisk together dashi, soy sauce, tamari, moromi miso, sake and mirin until well blended.

To serve Slice the tuna on a bias, then place it on a platter. Top it with shiro-negi and chives, then pour the sauce overtop.

Suggested wine Try a full-style vintage Champagne with a fine texture and flavours of brioche.

- 4 oz ahi (bigeye) tuna loin, cleaned
- 3½ Tbsp dashi (page 185)
- ¼ cup soy sauce
- 1½ Tbsp tamari
- 3 Tbsp moromi miso
- 4 Tbsp sake
- ⅓ cup mirin
- 1 tsp chopped chives
- 3 stalks shiro-negi (Japanese leek), thinly sliced lengthwise

Ahi Tuna Zuke

(Marinated Ahi Tuna)

SERVES 1

- 4 oz ahi (bigeye) tuna loin, cleaned
- 1 cup soy sauce
- 4-inch segment of daikon radish, peeled
- 4-inch segment of English cucumber, peeled
- 2 cups water
- 4 Tbsp salt
- 1/4 tsp wasabi paste

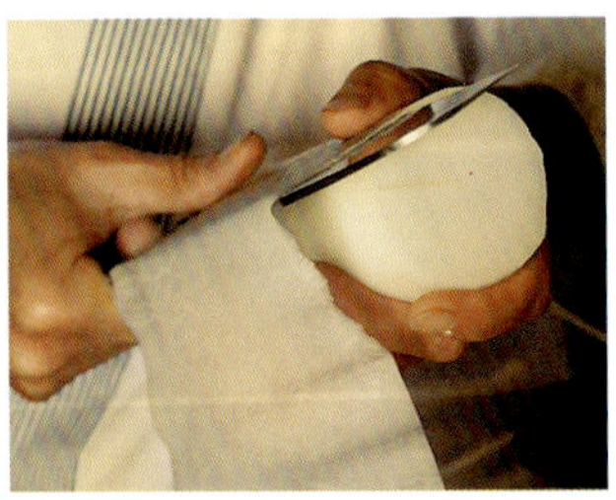

This recipe calls for a special cutting technique known as katsuramuki, *which allows you to produce long, thin sheets from cylindrical vegetables.*

In a small glass dish, cover tuna with soy sauce and allow to marinate for 30 minutes. Remove the tuna from the soy sauce and pat it dry.

As the tuna is marinating, cut a 6-inch sheet of daikon using the katsuramuki technique. To create a single sheet of daikon, insert a chef's knife just below the skin of the radish. Move the knife up and down in large strokes just under the surface and along the length of the daikon segment while rotating the radish. Continue cutting as smoothly and continuously as possible, using your thumb to regulate the thickness of the sheet as you cut. You should end up with a translucent, thin sheet of daikon 4 inches wide and 6 inches long. Repeat with the cucumber.

Combine water and salt in a small bowl. Add the daikon and cucumber sheets and soak for 30 minutes, then pat them dry.

Lay the daikon on a clean work surface, with the 4-inch side towards you. Place tuna on the daikon, as close to the bottom edge as possible. Starting at the bottom edge, tightly roll tuna in the daikon. Lay the cucumber sheet on the work surface, with the 4-inch side towards you. Place the daikon-wrapped tuna along the bottom edge of the cucumber sheet. Tightly roll up.

To serve Cut this roll into five pieces, arrange on a platter, dab with wasabi paste and serve.

Suggested wine Stay with crisp sauvignon blancs from the Loire or perhaps Central Otago.

Halibut Carpaccio

SERVES 1

- 4 oz halibut fillet, skin removed and deboned
- 1½ oz anchovies
- ¼ cup extra-virgin olive oil
- 2 to 3 cherry tomatoes, quartered
- 30 chervil leaves
- 2 shiso leaves, finely sliced

Ask your fishmonger for a firmer cut of halibut, preferably one close to the tail.

Lightly season halibut with salt and, using a kitchen torch, lightly sear fish for 2 minutes on each side. Finely slice the fish.

In a food processor, blend together anchovies and olive oil. Season to taste with pepper.

To serve Fan the halibut slices on a plate. Spread the anchovy mixture on top, then garnish with cherry tomatoes, chervil and shiso leaves.

Suggested wine Try a Carneros pinot gris, which would offer lively acidity and richness.

Gindara Yuanzuke

(Marinated Sablefish)

SERVES 4

- 1 cup soy sauce
- 1 cup sake
- 1 cup mirin
- 1 lb sablefish fillet, skin on but deboned
- 8 spears asparagus, woody ends trimmed
- 1 tsp mirin

Although the sablefish in this dish is broiled and therefore decidedly not raw, it belongs in this section because it is a quintessential Japanese dish.

In a medium bowl, combine soy sauce, sake and mirin. Cut sablefish into four equal portions and marinate them in the soy sauce mixture for 4 to 5 hours.

Preheat the broiler. Remove the fish from the sauce and broil it for 5 to 8 minutes, then turn the fish and broil for another 5 to 8 minutes until it is a light caramel colour. Remove from the heat and set aside.

Preheat a grill to high. Place asparagus on the grill, baste with the mirin and cook for 5 minutes.

To serve Slice asparagus in half and arrange on a plate. Top with the sablefish.

Suggested wine With such a strong marinade, go with a red with high acidity like a Dundee Hills pinot noir or a sharp Barbaresco.

Mirugai Ubuki Sashimi

(Geoduck Sashimi)

SERVES 4

Much of the heat in this dish comes from benitade, *or Japanese peppercress, which are tiny red sprouts with a slightly peppery taste, and from* karashi sumiso, *a mustard–miso vinegar mixture.*

- 1 large geoduck clam

Karashi sumiso

- 1 Tbsp tama miso (page 189)
- 1 tsp dry mustard powder
- Pinch of Japanese peppercress (benitade)
- 1 tsp rice vinegar

Bring a large pot of lightly salted water to a boil on high heat. Blanch geoduck for a mere 5 seconds, then remove from the water and cut the flesh out of the shell. Reserve the boiling water. Cut off the siphon (the long neck) and discard the rest. Peel off and discard the siphon's outer skin, then rinse it well and cut the siphon in half lengthwise.

Fill a large bowl with ice water. Using a very sharp knife, cut the siphon into dime-thick slices on a bias. Dip the slices into the boiling salted water for at most 1 second, then plunge them immediately into the ice bath.

Karashi sumiso In a small bowl, whisk together tama miso, mustard powder and peppercress. Measure 2 Tbsp of this paste and thin it with vinegar until the sauce reaches a creamy consistency.

To serve Arrange geoduck slices on a platter and serve the dipping sauce in a small bowl on the side.

Suggested wine A heavier sake will work here; try one that is unfiltered, such as Nigori.

Tsunami Kampachi Sashimi

(Hawaiian Yellowtail Sashimi)

SERVES 1 · SHOWN AT LEFT

Tosaka seaweed comes in three colours: green, red and white. The sheets come preserved in salt, so soak them in cold water for 5 minutes to remove the salt before adding them to the recipe. Yellowtail is now sustainably farmed in Kona, Hawaii. It is prized for its rich, delicious flavour and its firm yet succulent texture.

- 5 oz raw kampachi (yellowtail), skin removed, deboned and cut in 6 pieces
- 2 Tbsp soy sauce
- 2 Tbsp yuzu juice
- Dash of sesame oil
- 1 jalapeño pepper, seeded and sliced
- 1/4 oz to 1/2 oz fresh ginger, peeled and julienned
- 1/16 oz to 1/8 oz white tosaka seaweed

Using a kitchen torch, sear only one side of each piece of kampachi for 30 seconds. This process will tenderize the fish and give it a smoky flavour. Form each piece of fish into a roll and place it, seam-side down, on a plate.

In a bowl, combine soy sauce, yuzu juice and sesame oil.

To serve Top each piece of kampachi with a slice of jalapeño and julienned ginger. Garnish the side of the plate with the seaweed. Spoon the soy-yuzu sauce overtop and finish with a few drops of sesame oil to taste.

Suggested wine Try a high-quality dry sake with superior structure, such as Junmai-dai ginjo.

Kani Kaiware Salada

(Crab and Kaiware Salad)

SERVES 1

Kaiware are sprouts of daikon radish. You can find them at Asian supermarkets. This dish also calls for tobiko, flying fish roe, commonly used on sushi. Any fishmonger that sells sushi-grade fish should also be able to provide you with tobiko.

- 1 package kaiware (radish sprouts)
- 1 1/2 oz fresh crab meat, rinsed and picked over for small pieces of shell
- 1 red radish, sliced and soaked in cold water
- 1/2 oz tobiko (flying fish roe)
- 2 Tbsp ponzu shoyu (page 189)

Cut off and discard the roots of the kaiware, then cut the bunch in half. In a medium bowl, mix together kaiware, crab and radish.

To serve Sprinkle the salad with tobiko and add ponzu shoyu immediately before serving.

Suggested wine Try a richer riesling from Alsace, such as a Grand Cru Schlossberg.

Cold Uni Chawan Mushi

(Cold Uni Egg Custard)

SERVES 4

- 2 eggs
- 1⅔ cups dashi (page 185) + ½ cup for the sauce
- 4 tsp light soy sauce + extra for chawan mushi
- ¼ cup mirin + extra for chawan mushi
- 1 Tbsp Japanese potato starch (katakuri-ko) or cornstarch
- 8 sprigs mitsuba, stems only, in ¾-inch segments
- 12 pieces uni (2 sea urchins)

Mitsuba *is Japanese wild parsley, which is available from specialty food stores. If you cannot find it, use blanched snow peas that have been cut in half. Similarly, if you cannot find the clear* katakuri-ko, *a starch traditionally made from the corm of lilies but now often from potatoes, use white cornstarch in its place. This dish is traditionally made in chawan mushi cups; if you do not have any, use small ramekins instead.*

In a medium bowl, whisk together eggs and the 1⅔ cups of the dashi. Add 4 tsp soy sauce (or to taste), ¼ cup mirin (or to taste) and a pinch of salt. Pass the mixture through a fine-mesh sieve, then divide it among four chawan mushi cups. Cover the cups with lids and cook them in a steamer for 5 to 6 minutes. Remove them from the steamer and allow to cool to room temperature. Chill in the refrigerator for at least 30 minutes or until cold.

In a medium pot, combine the remaining ½ cup of dashi, 1 tsp of soy sauce and 1 tsp of mirin and heat over medium heat for 10 minutes. Dilute potato starch (or cornstarch) in a small amount of water until smooth, then add it gradually to the dashi mixture while stirring. When the mixture thickens and becomes smooth, remove it from the heat and allow to cool. Refrigerate this sauce for at least 10 minutes or until cold.

Fill a small bowl with ice water. Bring a small pot of water to a boil on high heat. Add mitsuba and blanch for 1 minute, then remove it from the pot and plunge it into the ice bath. Drain, then add it to the sauce.

To serve Place a chawan mushi cup on each of four plates. Spoon a quarter of the uni on top of each serving of custard, then pour the sauce overtop.

Suggested wine Try a vouvray or viognier, which will be rich and show a touch of sweetness.

Sushi Rice

MAKES 6 CUPS

To make sushi rice, it is best to use a wooden bowl called sushi-oke; *unfortunately, it is available only in large sizes for commercial use and must be ordered from Japan. You will also need a rice cooker for this recipe, as sticky rice burns very easily on the stove.*

- 3 cups water
- 1¾ lbs sushi rice
- 1 cup rice vinegar
- ¾ cup sugar
- 2 Tbsp salt

Combine water and rice in a large bowl, then strain it through a fine-mesh sieve. Repeat this washing and straining for 15 minutes. Place the water and rice in a rice cooker and allow to steam until the liquid is absorbed, 25 to 30 minutes.

To prepare sushi vinegar *(sushi-zu)*, mix vinegar, sugar and salt in a saucepan. Cook over low heat until the sugar dissolves, then remove from the heat and allow the mixture to cool.

Spread the hot steamed rice onto a large glass or ceramic plate or bowl. (Do not use metallic dishes as they may react with the rice vinegar.) Sprinkle the vinegar mixture over the rice and, using a *shamoji* (rice spatula), quickly and gently fold the vinegar into the rice. Be careful not to smash or cut the rice grains. As you mix the rice, fan it to cool it and remove its moisture. This will also give the rice a shiny look. Use sushi rice immediately. (Leftover sushi rice will keep in an airtight container at room temperature for 1 day.)

Rolling Sushi

Set a *makisu* (bamboo rolling mat) on a clean work surface and fully cover it with plastic wrap. Run your hands under cold running water to cool them (cold hands will sweat less and therefore stick less to the rice) and dry them well.

Place a sheet of nori seaweed on the makisu. Scoop up a small handful of sushi rice and shape it into a ball in your hands. Place the sushi rice in the centre of the nori and spread it out with your fingers to an even thickness of no more than ¼ inch, ensuring the entire sheet, including the corners, is well covered. Don't overwork the rice, as it will become like a paste.

Place the filling ingredients in a compact line in the centre of the rice. Fold the bottom of the nori sheet over the filling and roll up, pressing firmly on the makisu, into a solid log. Once you reach the end of the nori, press firmly and remove the makisu. The roll is now ready to be cut and served or to be topped with other ingredients as specified in the recipe.

Oyster Stamina Sushi

SERVES 1 · SHOWN AT UPPER RIGHT

Kabayaki sauce

- 2 Tbsp mirin
- 2 Tbsp sake
- 1 Tbsp + 1 tsp sugar
- 2 Tbsp + 1 tsp tamari
- 2 large Fanny Bay oysters (meat and liquor)

- 3/4 cup sushi rice (page 177)
- 1/2 sheet nori seaweed
- 2 slices cold smoked salmon
- 10 slices English cucumber
- 2 oz crab meat

Combine mirin and sake in a small pot. Boil over medium heat to evaporate alcohol. Be careful not to reduce the liquid completely. Add sugar and tamari and bring to a boil again. Add oyster meat and liquor and poach over very low heat for 3 minutes, turning the oysters over after 1½ minutes. Once oysters are springy to the touch, remove from liquid and set aside in a small bowl. Continue reducing sauce over medium heat until it starts to get syrupy. Pour reduction over poached oysters. Let sit for 10 minutes before cutting the oysters into thin slices. Reserve the leftover reduction.

Place nori on a makisu (rolling mat). Spread the rice over the nori, then turn the nori sheet upside-down, with the rice facing the makisu. Layer a 1-inch strip along one of the long edges with cold smoked salmon, cucumber and crab. Roll the sushi, following the instructions on page 177. Gently squeeze the roll so that it holds its shape. Remove the mat and place the oyster slices on top of the rice. Using the mat again, gently press the overlapping oyster slices onto the rice. Cut the roll into 8 slices and glaze oysters with leftover kabayaki sauce.

Suggested wine A lighter white wine will pair best with this sushi; try a crisp B.C. pinot gris or even a sauvignon blanc.

Caterpillar Sushi

SERVES 1 · SHOWN AT LOWER RIGHT

- 1/2 sheet nori seaweed
- 2 oz crab meat
- 10 slices of English cucumber
- 1/2 avocado, thinly sliced

One look at this lively roll is enough to understand how this sushi got its name.

Spread the crab meat over the nori sheet, leaving a 1-inch strip uncovered along one of the long edges. Layer this strip with cucumber and avocado. Using the *makisu* (rolling mat), tightly roll the sushi (see Rolling Sushi, page 177). Gently squeeze the roll so that it holds its shape. Cut the roll into 8 pieces.

To serve Place the pieces of caterpillar sushi on a plate and serve immediately.

Suggested wine Try an unfiltered sake with a fruity nose and a mild flavour, perhaps a nigori junmai.

King Crab Sushi

SERVES 1 · SHOWN AT LEFT

- 3/4 cup sushi rice
- 1/2 sheet nori seaweed
- 5 oz king crab meat
- 1 spear asparagus, blanched
- 10 slices English cucumber
- 1/4 oz kaiware (radish sprouts), roots trimmed and discarded
- 1 Tbsp sour cream
- 1 tsp tonburi (mountain caviar)

Spread the rice over the nori sheet, leaving a 1-inch strip uncovered along one of the long edges. Layer this strip with crab meat, asparagus, cucumber and kaiware. Using the *makisu* (rolling mat), tightly roll the sushi (see Rolling Sushi, page 177). Gently squeeze the roll so that it holds its shape. Cut the roll into 8 pieces.

To serve Place the pieces of crab sushi on a plate. Top each piece with a teaspoon of sour cream and some tonburi (page 40).

Suggested wine This sushi will work well with one of several different pairings: try a medium-dry sake of a junmai level or an unoaked chardonnay from California.

Sabazushi
(Mackerel Sushi)

SERVES 1

- 1 mackerel fillet, 8 oz, skin on
- 2 cups rice vinegar
- 2 pieces of battera seaweed
- 3/4 cup sugar
- 8 Sichuan pepper leaves (kinome)

Battera is a translucent seaweed that is available from specialty Japanese food stores. Kinome *are also known as Sichuan pepper leaves and they are tender leaves with a spicy, peppery taste.*

Cut the mackerel into three pieces lengthwise and heavily salt the fish. Allow to sit for 3 hours. Rinse off the salt with cold water and pat the fish dry with a paper towel. Transfer to a medium, nonreactive bowl, then add 1 cup of the vinegar and marinate for 30 minutes. Debone the mackerel and peel off the top layer of skin.

Place seaweed in a small pot with the remaining 1 cup of vinegar and cook on low heat for 30 minutes. Add sugar and cook 10 more minutes. Allow to cool at room temperature.

To serve Place the battera on the *makisu* (rolling mat). Arrange the mackerel on the battera sheet, leaving a 1-inch strip uncovered along one of the long edges. Layer this strip with Sichuan pepper leaves. Using the makisu, tightly roll the sushi (see Rolling Sushi, page 177). Gently squeeze the roll so that it holds its shape. Cut the roll into 8 pieces.

Suggested wine Try a sake of a junmai quality with medium dryness and lychee flavours.

BASICS

Vegetable Stock

MAKES 10 CUPS

- 4 Tbsp olive oil
- 2 large onions, chopped
- 3 leeks, white and light green parts, chopped
- 1 rib celery, chopped
- 2 large carrots, chopped
- ½ bulb garlic, peeled and chopped
- 1 bulb fennel, chopped
- 10 cups water
- 2 cups white wine
- 1 Tbsp black peppercorns
- 1 Tbsp coriander seeds
- 2 sprigs thyme
- 1 bay leaf
- 3 sprigs each parsley and chervil and 1 sprig tarragon, tied into a bouquet garni

In a wide stainless-steel pot, heat olive oil over medium heat. Add onions, leeks, celery, carrots, garlic and fennel and sauté until soft and fragrant but not browned, about 5 minutes. Add water and simmer for 15 minutes, then add wine and simmer for another 15 minutes. Add peppercorns, coriander seeds, thyme, bay leaf and bouquet garni and cook for a further 15 minutes. Remove the pot from the heat and allow to cool.

Fill a large roasting pan with ice. Strain the stock first through a colander and then through a fine-mesh sieve into a large bowl. Discard the solids. Set the bowl in the roasting pan and allow the stock to cool over ice until it reaches room temperature. Will keep refrigerated in an airtight container for up to 3 or 4 days.

Chicken Stock

MAKES 10 CUPS

- 3 chicken carcasses
- 1 chicken thigh
- 12 cups cold water
- 1 onion, chopped
- 1 leek, white and light green parts, chopped
- 1 carrot, chopped
- 1 rib celery, chopped
- 4 cloves garlic, chopped
- 2 sprigs thyme
- 1 bay leaf
- 3 sprigs each parsley and chervil and 1 sprig tarragon, tied into a bouquet garni

Cut up the chicken carcasses and thigh into 2-inch pieces and rinse them under cold running water for 10 minutes. Place them in a stockpot with the water and bring to a simmer on medium heat. Cook for 1 hour, skimming any impurities off the surface every 10 to 15 minutes. Do not stir the stock—doing so will result in a cloudy liquid. Add onion, leek, carrot, celery and garlic and simmer for 1 hour more. Carefully press any floating pieces of chicken or vegetables down into the stock with the back of a ladle. Add thyme, bay leaf and bouquet garni and cook for another 30 minutes.

Fill a large roasting pan with ice. Strain the stock first through a colander and then through a fine-mesh sieve into a large bowl. Discard the solids. Set the bowl in the roasting pan and allow the stock to cool until it reaches room temperature. Will keep refrigerated in an airtight container for up to 3 or 4 days.

Dark Chicken Stock

MAKES 10 CUPS

- 3 chicken carcasses
- 1 chicken thigh
- 1 onion, chopped
- 1 carrot, chopped
- 1 rib celery, chopped
- 4 cloves garlic, chopped
- 1 leek, white and light green parts, chopped
- 12 cups cold water
- 2 sprigs thyme
- 1 bay leaf
- 3 sprigs each parsley and chervil and 1 sprig tarragon, tied into a bouquet garni

Use this stock for dark-coloured sauces and jus. Light stocks are better for making soup bases or light-coloured sauces or for braising vegetables.

Preheat the oven to 350°F. Cut up chicken carcasses and thigh into 2-inch pieces and place them in a roasting pan. Cook in a convection oven for 25 minutes (45 minutes for a conventional oven) until the bones start to brown. Turn the pieces and roast for another 15 minutes. Add onion, carrot, celery and garlic and roast for 15 minutes.

Pour off the rendered fat and transfer the chicken pieces and roasted vegetables to a stockpot. Add leek and 6 cups of the water and cook over medium heat for 30 minutes until the liquid has reduced by half. Add the remaining 6 cups of water, thyme, bay leaf and bouquet garni and cook for an additional 30 minutes.

Fill a roasting pan with ice. Strain the stock first through a colander and then through a fine-mesh sieve into a large bowl. Discard the solids. Set the bowl in the roasting pan and allow the stock to cool until it reaches room temperature. Will keep refrigerated in an airtight container for up to 1 week.

Dashi

MAKES 8 CUPS

- 1 piece of dried kombu seaweed (about 12 inches long)
- 8 cups water
- 2 cups dried bonito flakes

Dashi is a basic Japanese stock made with kelp (kombu seaweed) and flakes from dried and smoked bonito (tuna) fish. You can find these ingredients at Asian supermarkets.

Wipe kombu gently with a moistened towel to remove any loose impurities. In a medium pot, combine kombu and water and bring to a simmer on medium-high heat. When the kombu rises to the surface, remove it from the pot. Turn off the heat, add bonito flakes and allow to infuse for 30 seconds. Use a spoon to skim any impurities off the surface.

Fill a large bowl with ice. Strain the broth immediately through a fine-mesh sieve into a medium bowl. Discard the solids. Set this bowl over the large bowl of ice and cool to room temperature. Will keep refrigerated in an airtight container for up to 1 week.

Fish Stock

MAKES 10 CUPS

- 4½ lbs fish bones and trimmings
- ¼ cup olive oil
- 1 large onion, chopped
- 1 leek, white and light green parts, chopped
- 2 ribs celery, chopped
- 2 fennel stalks, chopped
- ½ bulb garlic, peeled and chopped
- 2 cups dry white wine
- 3 sprigs thyme
- 1 bay leaf
- 2 sprigs parsley
- 12 cups cold water, or just enough to cover

The best fish to use for this fumet is a lean white fish such as halibut, striper bass or John Dory. Do not include the fish skin, and use fish heads only if you want a stronger stock, perhaps for fish soup, for example. If you do use fish heads, discard the gills first.

Cut fish bones and trimmings into 2-inch pieces and rinse them under cold running water for 10 to 15 minutes, then allow them to drain in a colander.

In a wide stainless-steel pot, heat olive oil on medium heat. Add onion, leek, celery, fennel and garlic and cook for about 5 minutes until soft and fragrant. Add the fish bones and trimmings and cook for 5 minutes, then add wine and bring the mixture to a boil. Add thyme, bay leaf, parsley and a pinch of salt. Add just enough cold water to cover the fish and vegetables. Reduce the heat to low and simmer the stock for 20 minutes, skimming any impurities off the surface every 5 minutes.

Fill a roasting pan with ice. Strain the stock first through a colander and then through a fine-mesh sieve into a plastic or stainless-steel bowl. Discard the solids. Set the bowl in the roasting pan and allow the stock to cool to room temperature. Will keep refrigerated in an airtight container for up to 5 days.

Ginger-scented Smoked Bonito Broth

MAKES 8 CUPS

- 1 piece of dried kombu seaweed (about 2 inches long)
- 8 cups cold water
- 2 dried shiitake mushrooms
- 2-inch piece of fresh ginger, peeled and thinly sliced
- ½ cup dried bonito flakes

This broth is a variation of dashi, flavoured with ginger and shiitake mushrooms.

Wipe kombu gently with a moistened towel to remove any loose impurities. Place it in a stockpot with water, mushrooms and ginger and bring to a slow simmer over medium heat. When the kombu rises to the surface, remove it from the pot. Turn off the heat, add bonito flakes and allow to infuse for 2 minutes. Use a spoon to skim any impurities off the surface.

Fill a large bowl with ice. Strain the stock through a fine-mesh sieve into a medium bowl. Discard the solids. Set this bowl over the large bowl of ice and cool to room temperature. Will keep refrigerated in an airtight container for up to 1 week.

White Wine Sauce

MAKES 1¾ CUPS

- 1 cup white wine
- 1 cup fish stock (page 186)
- 4 shallots, minced
- 4 oz button mushrooms, thinly sliced
- ½ cup whipping cream
- 1 cup unsalted butter, cold, cubed

This sauce can be used as a base for any fish dish.

In a medium saucepan, combine wine, fish stock, shallots and mushrooms and heat on medium heat until liquid has reduced by three-quarters, 10 to 15 minutes. Add cream, bring the mixture to a simmer, then whisk in the butter a bit at a time until well emulsified. Strain this sauce through a fine-mesh sieve into a clean bowl and season with salt and pepper. Discard any solids. Will keep refrigerated in an airtight container for up to 10 days.

Beurre Blanc

MAKES 1 CUP

- 2 shallots, minced
- ¼ cup white wine
- 2 Tbsp white wine vinegar
- 5 black peppercorns
- 1 cup unsalted butter, cold, cubed

This is a simple, light sauce that is perfect for seafood, shellfish and vegetable dishes.

In a small saucepan, combine shallots, wine, vinegar and peppercorns. Heat on medium heat until liquid has reduced by three-quarters, 10 to 15 minutes. Reduce the heat to low, then whisk in cold butter a bit at a time until well emulsified. Strain the butter mixture through a fine-mesh sieve, discard the solids and season with salt and pepper.

Ponzu Shoyu

MAKES 15 CUPS

- 7¼ cups ponzu sauce
- 7¼ cups soy sauce
- 1½ oz kombu seaweed (about 4 inches long)
- 1½ oz bonito flakes

Use this sauce as a seasoning for tataki-style or sashimi-style dishes.

Combine all of the ingredients in an airtight container and refrigerate for 1 week. Strain the liquid through a fine-mesh sieve or cheesecloth into a small bowl, discarding the solids. Will keep refrigerated in an airtight container for up to 2 weeks.

Tosazu Sauce

MAKES 5 CUPS

- 3 cups dashi (page 185)
- 1¼ cups rice vinegar
- ⅓ cup soy sauce
- ⅓ cup mirin
- ⅓ oz dried bonito flakes

This sauce is best served with sunomono salad.

Combine dashi, vinegar, soy sauce and mirin in a large pot and bring to a boil on high heat. Turn off the heat, add bonito flakes and allow to infuse for 2 minutes. Skim any impurities that float to the surface. Strain the sauce through a fine-mesh sieve or a cheesecloth into a small bowl, discarding the solids. Will keep refrigerated in an airtight container for up to 1 week.

Tama Miso

MAKES 3 CUPS

- 1 lb shiro miso (white miso paste)
- 3 egg yolks
- ½ cup mirin
- ½ cup sake
- ½ cup sugar
- ¼ cup sesame paste

Whisk together all ingredients in a medium pot. Heat on low heat, whisking constantly, until the mixture becomes smooth and shiny, about 15 minutes. Pass the mixture through a fine-mesh sieve into a medium bowl. Will keep refrigerated in an airtight container for up to 1 week.

CONVERSION CHARTS

Weight

(rounded to nearest even whole number)

Imperial	Metric
1 oz	28 g
2 oz	58 g
3 oz	86 g
4 oz	114 g
5 oz	142 g
6 oz	170 g
7 oz	198 g
8 oz (½ lb)	226 g
9 oz	256 g
10 oz	284 g
11 oz	312 g
12 oz	340 g
13 oz	368 g
14 oz	396 g
15 oz	426 g
16 oz (1 lb)	454 g

Volume

(rounded to closest equivalent)

Imperial	Metric
⅛ tsp	0.5 mL
¼ tsp	1 mL
½ tsp	2.5 mL
¾ tsp	4 mL
1 tsp	5 mL
1 Tbsp	15 mL
1½ Tbsp	25 mL
⅛ cup	30 mL
¼ cup	60 mL
⅓ cup	80 mL
½ cup	125 mL
⅔ cup	160 mL
¾ cup	180 mL
1 cup	250 mL

Liquid

(rounded to closest equivalent)

Imperial	Metric
1 oz	30 mL
1½ oz	45 mL
2 oz	60 mL
3 oz	90 mL
4 oz	120 mL
6 oz	180 mL
8 oz	240 mL

Linear

(rounded to closest equivalent)

Imperial	Metric
⅛ inch	3 mm
¼ inch	6 mm
1 inch	2.5 cm
1¼ inches	3 cm
6 inches	15 cm
8 inches	20 cm
9 inches	22.5 cm

Temperature

(rounded to closest equivalent)

Imperial	Metric
150°F	65°C
160°F	70°C
175°F	80°C
200°F	95°C
225°F	105°C
250°F	120°C
275°F	135°C
300°F	150°C
325°F	160°C
350°F	180°C
375°F	190°C
400°F	205°C
425°F	220°C
450°F	230°C
475°F	245°C
500°F	260°C

blue water cafe
+ raw bar

ACKNOWLEDGEMENTS

Much praise is due the dedicated team at Blue Water Cafe and the passionate, gifted individuals who lead that team: Frank Pabst, Stephan Cachard, Masaaki Kudo, Benjamin Wristen, Adrien Boutet, Jean-Pierre Sanchez, William Mulholland, Colin MacDougall, Cara Dunlop and Marilyn Woo. Thanks also go to the restaurant's alumni for their contributions, principally James Walt. I would also like to thank Lawrence Fung, Neil Henderson, Lynn Gervais and Min Jee from Toptable Group, Jamie Maw, and the late Werner Forster, whose legacy is the unique blend of old and new in the restaurant's design.

Of course, of special mention is Jack Evrensel, without whose vision and passion none of this would have been attainable. As in our first book, the restaurant has been brought to life in these pages by John Sherlock's brilliant photography and Jim Tobler's eloquent prose.

This book is also a testament to conscientious choices in dining. We want to thank every individual who has, by sharing the experience at Blue Water Cafe, supported the decisions made by Frank and amplified our day-by-day effort to sustain our world's ocean food resources.

MICHAEL DOYLE
President
Toptable Group

blue water cafe
FRANK PABST
EXECUTIVE CHEF

INDEX

Photos are referenced in italics